Socrates at Verse

SOCRATES AT VERSE

and Other Philosophical Poems

Christopher Norris

Parlor Press
Anderson, South Carolina
www.parlorpress.com

Parlor Press LLC, Anderson, South Carolina, 29621

Printed in the United States of America
S A N: 2 5 4 - 8 8 7 9

Library of Congress Cataloging-in-Publication Data on File

978-1-64317-159-3 (paperback)
978-1-64317-160-9 (PDF)
978-1-64317-161-6 (ePub)

1 2 3 4 5

Cover design by David Blakesley.
Cover art:
Printed on acid-free paper.

Parlor Press, LLC is an independent publisher of scholarly and trade titles in print and multimedia formats. This book is available in paperback and ebook formats from Parlor Press on the World Wide Web at http://www.parlorpress.com or through online and brick-and-mortar bookstores. For submission information or to find out about Parlor Press publications, write to Parlor Press, 3015 Brackenberry Drive, Anderson, South Carolina, 29621, or email editor@parlorpress.com.

for Val

Contents

Contents

Foreword

This is a collection of poems all written over the past three years or so, all of them markedly formal in character (that is, rhymed and metrical), and often on philosophical or philosophy-related themes. Some have to do with the lives and works of individual thinkers from Socrates, Descartes, Hume and Kant to Kierkegaard, Nietzsche, Wittgenstein, Adorno and Derrida. Others offer thoughts – arguments, even – about a wide range of topics including time, Platonism, promises, idealism, aesthetics, free-will *versus* determinism, moral character, animals, quantum theory, rule-following, and philosophy of mathematics. Others again are less overtly philosophical in character but make the case – or express and embody my preference – for a poetry that does currently unfashionable things such as discussing, debating, objecting, controverting, and (in short) arguing. There are several pieces that have to do with aspects of literature and music but earn a place here because, as so often from Socrates down, they come at their themes through a broaching of topics in literary theory and musicology. Other poems have topics of a more everyday, personal or anecdotal interest that likewise engage in the fundamental business of thinking things through – feelings and emotions included – as clearly as possible without understating the complexities involved.

The rhyme schemes and metrical patterns are varied but have enough in common, formally speaking, to unite the poems across some otherwise large contrasts of treatment and tone. Implicit throughout is my central claim: that poetic thinking is distinctive – and philosophizing in verse a worthwhile activity – in so far as it operates within certain constraints that can themselves become springboards for the exercise of intellectual creativity. More than that, they can serve to focus attention on philosophical or other sorts of issue by means not available to straightforward discursive prose.

Most obvious among them is the old chestnut of free will *versus* determinism, here brought up in a variety of contexts from quantum mechanics to mathematics, memory, cognitive psychology, and probability theory. The analogy I am suggesting – the way that verse calls for a high degree of inventive freedom even (or especially) where constrained by exigencies of poetic form – is a theme, or more often a running subtext, in many of these poems. It could only come across to convincing effect in a poetry that shares certain basic intellectual, reflective and discursive resources with the language and the thought-procedures of communicative prose.

When Archibald MacLeish famously said, in his verse-essay 'Ars Poetica' (1926), that 'a poem should not mean/But be', he was putting a case later taken up and dogmatically reinforced by numerous poets and critics with their proto-antecedents in Romanticism and French Symbolism and their proximate source in Anglo-American Modernism. It was always a decidedly leaky sort of dogma with prohibited stuff seeping in from history, author-biography, philosophy, cultural context, and other such presumptively illicit sources. Besides, MacLeish's own statement self-deconstructs on the point that it is, precisely, *a statement* and subject to the operative terms and conditions of constative – reason-giving, critically evaluable – discourse. (One could say that he is writing a verse-essay, not a poem, but that would beg the question against those, like me, who don't accept the distinction as framed in such a strongly binary and ideologically laden form.) My poems thus take aim at the notion – often the fixed prejudice – that poems should not argue, state a case, or do the kind of thing that other (i.e., prosaic or discursive) language-forms typically do. Roland Barthes once wrote, in a different but related connection, that 'a little formalism takes one away from history, but a lot of formalism brings one back to it'. I would add: the good formalism (the large-dose variety) is good just because what it lacks in doctrinal muscle it makes up for in subtlety, applicable range, and openness precisely to that which eludes any prior formulation of what counts as 'form'.

The more doctrinaire version is nowadays deeply ingrained among poets and critics, to the extent that it pretty much defines the orthodoxy on topics such as metaphor, symbol, poetic voice, genre, and of course the poetry/prose distinction. It is a partisan, creatively restrictive and intellectually incapacitating doctrine which has produced, along with some striking individual achievements, a good deal of mediocre and some actively harmful writing. By 'harmful' I mean the modern trend toward a poetry that narrows its sights to the point of fixation on its own, often private or scarcely communicable feelings. Another aim here is to contest the present-day hegemony of lyric, or the largely unquestioned idea that modes of first-person, intensely subjective or (at the extreme) confessional poetry are and should be the norm. The last stage of this retreat into navel-gazing or morbid self-obsession is memorably, if lamely, described in the lines from William Wordsworth's stuffed-owl favorite 'Resolution and Independence': 'We poets in our youth begin in gladness;/But thereof come in the end despondency and madness'.

Its results were laid out for part-clinical, part-cautionary, and part-celebratory inspection in Al Alvarez's 1972 book *The Savage God: a study of suicide*. This includes a distinctly ambivalent meditation on the poetry, life and death of Sylvia Plath, along with kindred reflections on the cases of John Berryman, Robert Lowell and others, all taken to merit – for better or worse – his none the less admiring, even awe-struck description of them as 'Extremist' poets. Whatever one's assessment of their, or his, work it is surely worth querying this equation between poetic-imaginative depth and insight on the one hand and, on the other, a subjective intensity measured by its more or less resolutely risking madness and/or suicide. It is a mischievous and dangerous creed, as well as having led to many critical misjudgments based on an over-valuation of strong (sometimes inchoate) feelings and an under-valuation of form, technique, intelligence, and verse-music.

I added the last term with pointed intent since the verbal music of a well-crafted formal poem is strictly inseparable from those other three qualities. Certain sorts of verse-music, especially the plangent or melancholy sorts, when combined with impressive formal technique but without very much in the way of self-critical or reflective intelligence – as often with the poems of A.E. Housman – can leave the reader feeling intellectually and even ethically short-changed. However the opposite is also the case, as Groucho Marx used to say: technique, form and wit will alike be wasted on poetry that lacks verse-music, whether of a melancholy, lively, haunting or subtly ambivalent character. The confusion gets in, I think, when critics talk about 'music' but when their claims can best be construed as referring to a variously weighted combination of prosodic, syntactic, phonetic, phonemic, and semantic attributes. My poems have a good deal to say on this topic, whether (occasionally) as a matter of overt theme or, more often, by way of self-reflexive implication. At any rate there is more going on with verse-music than could ever be explained by theories that detach 'musical' elements like rhyme, alliteration, assonance and so forth from those other, meaning-related or conceptually pertinent domains.

Nor can it be held distinct from the kinds of linguistically manifest intelligence that manage to do inventive, suggestive, metaphorically striking, or (in Heidegger's depth-hermeneutic parlance) 'world-disclosive' things with words. Verse-music of the 'pure' sort, in so far as it exists, is more like those sonorous and ear-beguiling though often boomily vacuous aspects of Tennyson's poetry picked up by Victorian 'nonsense' rhymesters such as Edward Lear and Lewis Carroll. And indeed, any mention of Heidegger in this regard should be qualified by noting that there is something problematic – something decidedly *un*intelligent – about his appeal to the etymological roots of certain, for the most part ancient Greek or modern German words as an index of their special truth-telling virtue. Such ideas are always in danger of promoting, as they do in his case, a nationalist mystique of origins and a creed of cultural-linguistic predestination with drastically prescriptive claims on the poet's or the philosopher-critic's freedom. To this extent Heidegger's account of poetry and its role in world-disclosure, or 'unconcealment', goes directly against what I have said about the role of active, inventive poetic thought.

This seems to be the gist when literary critics speak of poetry – especially the poetry they most value – as 'creative-exploratory' or as somehow achieving, in a short space of utterance, what natural languages achieve over much greater lengths of socio-cultural evolution. Back in the day, when I wrote academic literary theory and then continentally-inclined philosophy, I took inspiration from two of the most extravagantly gifted critic-philosophers of recent times, William Empson and Jacques Derrida. What they shared, despite huge differences in other ways, was a marvelously sensitive ear for nuances of sense and tone, an exceptionally keen analytical intelligence, and a manner of writing (the phrase is inadequate but I shy away from Derridean *écriture* in deference to Empson) that lives up creatively to that which it discovers in literary or other kinds of text. I hope that at least a few of these poems will come across to readers as offering examples of that two-way, mutually stimulating process at work.

Swansea, Wales
December 2019

Acknowledgments

I am grateful in many ways to numerous people, among them Heike Bauer, David Jonathan Bayot, Pete Boxall, Joe Brooker, Terry Eagleton, Tim Evans, Niall Gildea, Martin Gollan, Anita Walia Harris, Rahim and Wendy Hassan, Ric Hool, Rebekah Humphreys, Paddy Jemmer, Mike Jenkins, Peter Thabit Jones, Phil Knight, Peter Lamarque, Rebecca Lowe, Alan Morrison, Jolan Orban, Marianna Papastephanou, Mike Quille, David and Emily Rothman, Susan Spears, Rhoda Thomas, Manuel Barbeito Varela, and Sue Wiseman. My wife Valerie was hugely generous with help and support, as well as offering some great renditions of various poems on sundry, more or less public occasions and putting up with lengthy periods of silent absorption on my part.

Socrates at Verse

Bishop Berkeley's Apology

*That there is no such thing as what philosophers call material
substance, I am seriously persuaded: but if I were made to see any
thing absurd or sceptical in this, I should then have the same rea-
son to renounce this, that I imagine I have now to reject the con-
trary opinion.*

George Berkeley,
Three Dialogues between Hylas and Philonous

*Berkeley, after abolishing matter, is only saved from complete sub-
jectivism by a use of God that most subsequent philosophers have
regarded as illegitimate.*

Bertrand Russell,
A History of Western Philosophy

Mere common sense, though mostly thought absurd.
Mere common sense,
        though it was quite a while
Before my first few acolytes concurred.

All down to Locke, my world-upending style!
All down to Locke,
        my wrecking the pretence
Of realist types to go that extra mile.

Though he demurred, I jumped right off the fence.
Though he demurred
        for fear the realists mock,
I came right out and broke the thought-suspense.

Let me not smile at this, their state of shock.
Let me not smile
        as the Locke-tutored herd
Of *faux*-empiricists reel from the dock.

Their recompense? To grasp what I inferred!
Their recompense?
          to grasp that minds compile
No world-accompt till by the senses stirred.

The real's in hock to our sense-data file!
The real's in hock
          to our not knowing whence
They come, those semblances that so beguile.

An otiose third, the realist's last defence.
An otiose third,
          that trick devised to block
The void beyond what hints God might dispense.

How then make trial, how take your realist stock?
How then make trial
          of whether that fine word,
'Reality', kicks back like solid rock?

Sound thoughts commence with what's seen, felt, or heard.
Sound thoughts commence
          with God to reconcile
The rift those Lockeans tacitly averred.

The realist flock deem such talk puerile.
The realist flock
          deny my evidence
That *real*'s a reading off the sensory dial.

Be not deterred by jests at our expense.
Be not deterred;
          there's no hole they can knock
In truths God-vouched through human sentience.

Socrates at Verse: a life redeemed

The same dream came to me often in my past life: 'Socrates,' it said, 'make music and work at it'. And I formerly thought that, just as people encourage runners by cheering, so the dream was encouraging me to do what I was doing, that is, to make music, because philosophy was the greatest kind of music. But now, after the trial and while the festival of the god delayed my execution, I thought, in case the repeated dream really meant to tell me to make that which is ordinarily called music, I ought to do so and not to disobey. . . . So first I composed a hymn to the god whose festival it was; and after the god, considering that a poet, if he is really to be a poet, must compose myths and not speeches, since I was not a maker of myths, I took the myths of Aesop, which I had at hand and knew, and turned into verse the first I came upon.

Plato,
Phaedo, trans. Harold North Fowler, Sections 60d-61b

Versifying Aesop explicitly makes Socrates a poet, though his philosophical pursuits and verbal artistry would have qualified him as a poet in a less technical sense; Alcibiades refers to him as a Marsyas, a maker of supernaturally beguiling music.

Todd M. Compton,
Victim of the Muses

My friends, you find me at a time when death's
Now certain prospect leaves me less inclined
To spend my few remaining mortal breaths

On those old topics you've no doubt a mind
To raise once more. Back then, we'd spend our days
And half our nights on questions of a kind

To lead us puzzlers into such a maze
Of doubts and paradoxes that we'd keep
On finding yet more convoluted ways

To make sure no-one ever got to sleep
Before the small hours. Let's be very clear:
Those questions take the concept-diver deep

As thinking goes so I'll say nothing here
That means disowning the 'old' Socrates,
Your mentor, friend, instructor, and (since we're

All seekers after truth through the degrees
Of soul-perfection from erotic love
To spiritual) the lover whom you'd please,

And who'd please you, with apt reminders of
That heavenward ascent. So don't construe
This change in me as showing I'm 'above'

(Whatever that could mean) those things that drew
Us all together, that were my and your
Great portals of discovery, and through

Whose sovereign influence we sophomore
Enquirers learned at last to recognise
The ignorance we'd managed to ignore

In our old mental torpor. Yet, surprise
Or shock you as it may, I lately crave
Some less cerebral way to exercise

My wits than dialectics, that which gave
Such pleasure once, and does so still, though now,
I tend to think, the pleasure that a slave-

Boy – like the one I taught so quickly how
To reason like Pythagoras – might take
In mental operations that allow

The rudest of mechanicals to make
The cleverest moves.
                    You're wondering just what
Strange revelation I'm about to break

On your bewildered souls, or what new plot-
Twist in the tangled narrative we've shared
Through all my ploys to put you on the spot,

Elenchus-wise, and show just how you'd erred
Along the way, though always – don't forget –
Conceding that we're intimately paired,

'Teacher' and 'acolyte', in the duet
Of knowing and unknowing. Now it's my
Whole sense of things that's changed and somehow let

Those feelings loose that hitherto I'd try
To rein in like the wild, unruly horse
Of unregenerate instinct mastered by

The pure-bred steed of reason, or the force
Of better argument. That image (mine,
Set down by scribbler Plato) has its source

In thoughts that future scholars may assign
To its apprentice status or, instead,
To some late-onset cognitive decline,

With both hypotheses designed to head
Off one main charge. Thus: my ideas, in truth,
Were mere poetic metaphors, all 'fed

And watered by the passions', hence uncouth
Enough or bucking-bronco-like to earn
My own old quip that tied them to the youth

Of humankind. Then poets who could turn
A memorable line or striking piece
Of imagery were reckoned fit to churn

Out stuff that hymned the glory that was Greece
In verse-forms shrewdly chosen to conceal
Its origins in fantasy, caprice,

And – the base coin in which those hucksters deal –
'Poetic licence'. There you have the gist
Of how I used to think, or maybe feel,

Since that distinction blurs once you resist
My student Plato's over-zealous drive
To turn my rough-cast pairs into a list

Of type-cast binaries. They treat what I've
Set up by way of figurative aid-
To-thought as if all thinking should connive

At placing some immovable blockade
Twixt thought and feeling, reason and the voice
Of those profound emotions that persuade

The soul to higher things when they rejoice
The empathetic heart.
            So here I stand
Before you, one whom fate allows no choice

But death, yet who'll now meet it flute in hand,
A text of Aesop's Fables within reach,
And, thus equipped, a will so to expand

The scope of his soul-faculties that each
Becomes a microcosm wherein all
Can find their own perfection. If I'd teach

You one thing it's the need to overhaul
Your prejudices, even those that seem
Like edicts of the Logos, and to call

Time on those fixed priorities you deem
Self-evident. For then they might turn out
To strike you that way only on some scheme

Of values that, as soon as placed in doubt,
Could leave you marvelling why you ever took
The self-denying path that brought about

Your single-minded will to overlook
So many fine endeavours in pursuit
Of one remote ideal. What really shook

My old devotion to the absolute
In all its tempting guises was the thought
Of how a slave-girl's fingering on the flute,

So sinuous and sweet, could leave me wrought
To heights of passion scarcely to be borne,
As if against all reason I'd been caught

And spirited beyond the Gate of Horn
To some uncharted region. Now the lure
Of dialectic struck a note forlorn

On ears so lately tuned to that impure
Yet soul-regaling music that requires
We cease inventing fictions to assure

King Nous his throne amongst the dreaming spires.
Should Plato challenge, just tip him the wink
That maybe it's the sound of flutes and lyres,

Expertly played, that gives us most to think
Concerning the inseparable bond
Of soul and body, or those notes that link

Our sensuous lives with all that points 'beyond'
Their realm (as once I thought) and bids us quit
The body's soul-befuddling demi-monde

For such angelic pleasures as befit
Our higher selves. Once through that entrance-test
We're Plato's progeny, trained to outwit

All comers in the contest for who's best
At a well-turned elenchus, or who scores
Most points in argument when hardest pressed,

Or who comes out top player in those wars
Of dialectic cunning.
                    Not for me
That old mind-country from whose native shores

I've now set sail well knowing this will be
My final voyage, one that oddly leads
From soul to body just when they decree,

Those wise Athenians, that my misdeeds –
Or youth-corrupting words – require that soul
Should part from body. Thus the state proceeds

With its new policy of thought-control
By means, I'm bound to say, that aren't so far
Removed from those deployed in my old role

As elenchist-in-chief and commissar
For making sure that no ephebe of mine
Should hitch his errant wagon to the star

Of sensuous ecstasy. Else it might shine
So bright that reason's distant glimmer fell
On eyes too tired or dazzled to divine

The ideal truth of things, such was the spell
That music cast. Her flute it was that had
This curious effect and, strange to tell,

The thought of death close-up that made me glad
To chance on Aesop's Fables in a text,
A prose rendition, that I found a tad

Banausic. This I opted, as my next
Stint of conversion therapy, to cast
In verse just like the exercise that vexed

Me as a school-boy when, five decades past,
I had to turn the same prosodic trick
But in reverse.
            I know you'll say 'At last

Old Socrates has had the sense to kick
His philosophic hang-ups and accept
That he, like everyone, can only click

With less-than-willing listeners if they're swept
Away, once in a while at least, by flights
Of metaphor. Else it requires they're prepped

With allegories and figures that by rights,
On your official theory, would attract
Stern censure from the intellectual heights,

Though your reported discourses are packed
With those fixed staples of the poet's art
That showed, on your submission, how they lacked

All claim to truth or reason'. For my part,
And setting old controversies aside
(What need that I, death-marked, should still outsmart

Those who'll live on to witness how I died?),
There's this one point I'd bring in self-defence
Against the charge of having first denied,

And then late on, no doubt in recompense,
Affirmed and, by example, held sublime
The poet's special gift. He'll so condense

Our conjoint thoughts and feelings that, when I'm
Beneath that wondrous spell, I can't conceive
Why I devoted so much of my time

To coming up with arguments that leave
Me now not merely unconvinced but just
Flat-out amazed that ever I could weave

Such flimsy pretexts for a breach of trust
With shared humanity. For that's our means
Of accessing what ultimately must,

I've come to think, elude the fixed routines
Of any dialectic strictly trained
On a thought-strategy that intervenes

Whenever we suspect that feeling's gained
An edge through metaphor's seductive power.
Then intellect pronounces 'charge sustained'

In cases where the charge comes down to our
Flesh-frailty in preferring words that catch
A glimpse of rainbow in the Summer shower

We see and feel to words that seek a match
Between abstractions perfectly devoid
Of living speech. For otherwise they'd snatch

It back, that glimpse, as something once enjoyed
Beyond prosaic telling yet revealed
Or shown in ways that, years back, I deployed

All my best arguments to drive out-field
But which now seem to me the only hope
Of making good the promise long concealed

In poetry: to do by way of trope,
Of image, allegory, and all their kin
What lies intrinsically beyond the scope

Of unassisted reason.
                    You'll begin,
At this point, to remind me of the case
I once brought forward: how the poet's sin

Consisted first in giving pride of place
To fictions (that is, outright lies disguised
In fictive form); then, second, in the space

This left for modes of mimesis devised
To fool the naïve reader; and, my third
And major charge, in how it advertised

Those passions that a wiser soul deterred
Since all too apt to steer that soul astray
As might unruly winds a migrant bird

Caught far from home. All this I used to say
With full conviction and, I freely own,
A passion of the abstract kind that they,

My followers, took to set the proper tone
For any discourse meriting the name
Of true philosophy. But I've been thrown

So far from my old landmarks, like that same
Disoriented bird, that now I find
Great pleasure, challenge, and no cause for shame

In versifying Aesop's tales, designed
(I've come to think) not just to give the kids
Rich entertainment artfully combined

With moral lessons but – my Daimon bids
Me tell you now – to show truths that surpass
Those rules by which the dialectic rids

Itself of errors that a first-year class
In logic should sort out. And, friends, there's this
To add: that sometimes 'seeing in a glass,

Though darkly', as they say, can mean we miss
The literal or superficial drift
Yet glimpse beneath it, as when buds dehisce,

What constitutes the poet's greatest gift
To us philosophers as much as those,
The visionaries and dreamers, who would lift

Our questing intellects above the prose
Of logic-chopping reason and so bring
Our souls that inner harmony that goes

With conflicts overcome. It was my sting,
My gadfly buzzing, that they so reviled,
Those fellow-citizens who'd rather cling

To false beliefs and every sort of wild-
Eyed prophecy thrown up when they'd consult
Their dodgy oracles and those self-styled

Soothsayers. Better they, as suits adult,
Not childish minds, let reason bring to bear
Its murk-dispelling light on such occult

Reminders of the human love-affair
With any nonsense that gives half a chance
For fools and charlatans to stick with their

Absurd conceptions. Thus my favoured stance
Was that of a *provocateur* who'd prod
And tease them, get them moving to a dance

Of nimble dialectics, with the odd
Sideways allusion to their old ideas
Lest, gods forfend, I seemed to ride roughshod

Over the deep-entangled hopes and fears
That found in such beliefs a means to still
Mock-monsters lurking close to the frontiers

Of their untutored minds.
                    That's why I'd drill
It into them, the need that they engage
Brain before speaking, or mistrust the skill

In speech by which shrewd orators upstage
Deep thinkers and seduce the mind in thrall
To superstitious notions that assuage

The fearful for a while but then appal
Them all the more for conjuring a realm
Of false or fictive entities on call

Whenever old compulsions overwhelm
Their ill-defended minds. But now I've come
To think that having reason at the helm

So constantly might strike the Logos dumb,
Or that the real effect of all my gad-
Fly tricks was not to quicken but to numb

That sense of deeper insights to be had
From poetry and music than the sort
Of thing that we, in our Olympiad

For agile minds, took as our favourite sport
Or mental exercise. Thus we deprived
Ourselves of dialectic's sole resort

When it runs out of strategies contrived
To keep its end up and disguise its lack
Of any substance beyond that derived

From getting some smart-ass rejoinder back
Each time that I, or one of you, produced
Some thesis that required a shift of tack

On the opponent's part. So we got used
To playing a continual game of wits
As if the spectacle of someone goosed

By someone else, or forced to call it quits,
Must be what all philosophers most seek
To lay before us and what best befits

The name 'philosophy'.
        Of course I speak
As one who's done more than his share to spread
That strange idea of thinking-as-technique

Plus all the fallacies to which it led,
Like counting mere analysis the one
Sure path to truth, or urging we should shed

The veil of physical appearance, shun
All bodily affections, and aspire
To rid ourselves of the illusions spun

By poets. Hence their inchoate desire
That words take sensuous shape yet circumvent
And so transcend the sensory cave and fire

Whose flickerings, as I used to think, present
A shadow-play 'reality' divorced
From that which true philosophers frequent

Since their ideal conceptions are outsourced
To some transcendent realm of perfect Forms,
Ideas, or Essences. The claim's endorsed

By reason with its anhedonic norms
But lacks assurance should one think to ask,
As I do now: what price the endless swarms

Of sense-delighting input that they task
Themselves, those poor ascetics, to erase
From memory? Yet this can barely mask

The psychic conflict in a speech that pays
High tribute to the soul-perfecting good
Of theory or abstraction, yet betrays

In every passing metaphor what should,
By its own lights, be labelled out-of-bounds
For anyone who's truly understood

The need that reason not appeal to grounds
Beyond itself. For its best practice owns
No lingering fealty to the sights and sounds

That captivate with figural overtones
And so contrive, it cautions, to mislead
The word-enchanted listener into zones

Of verbal disrepute. Here monsters breed
As reason gives mere rhetoric free rein
To work its sundry mischiefs without heed

To disciplines of thought that might restrain
Such fancy-flights before they come to grief
Like Icarus, legs kicking from the main

And none the wiser.
                Such was my belief
Back then when I persuaded you to share
My logocentric bias and, in brief,

To spend your lives in stellar regions where
Such discourse was the only pastime left
Us mind-space dwellers used to the thin air

Of dialectic. So we lived bereft
Of just those attributes that most regale
The soul in quest of means to heal the cleft

Between a mind dead set to countervail
The body's vital force while senses brace
Against mind's strategies to tip the scale

Back in its favour. That's the choice we face
As heaven-gazers if we don't take note
Of that which tickled pink the Maid of Thrace

When Thales – all we have's the anecdote
But it rings true – fell into a deep hole,
So keen was our precursor to devote

His undistracted focus to the sole
Concern of plotting a celestial map.
Thus he had broken limbs to bear the toll

Of absent-mindedness or take the rap
For soul's enslavement to the rarified
Or star-struck speculations that could wrap

A thinker up so deeply as to hide
The pit before his feet.
                    But why, you've yet
To ask, that transformation by which I'd

Come round so late to feeling such regret
For all those – I'll not call them 'lost decades',
But decades spent in running up a debt

Of soul to sense? It's a mind-state that trades
The pleasures of a sensuous delight
In poetry or music for the shades

Of intellect and the ascetic blight
Inflicted by a doctrine that denies
The sense-modalities of sound and sight

Their role as the essential ears and eyes
Of intellect itself. So now you know:
Your teacher Socrates, who'd once advise

Strict rationing of all the things that go
To stimulate our senses, now commends
Not only those blest intervals we owe

To music that miraculously blends
The sensuous and the soulful but, as you
Should soon discover for yourselves, my friends,

The mental benefits that may accrue
From even (you may think) so artisan
Or technical a craft as I pursue

When turning Aesop into lines that scan
And make of his improving moral tales
A verbal music more uplifting than

The plain-prose version. Not that Aesop fails
To move and stir us as each story points
Its moral message in a way that nails

The rogues, cuts human nature at the joints,
And leaves us errant mortals better placed
To judge which animal the tale anoints

Its spokesman for a value-system based
On shrewd self-interest mixed with just a touch
Of mutual feeling lest the reader's taste

For high-toned messages revolt at such
A low-toned upshot. Yet it's no mere whim,
This wish of mine to versify as much

Of Aesop's homely stuff as I can trim
To hexametric form and so deter
The eye or ear from any wish to skim

The tale for some trite moral, or concur
Unthinkingly with its simplistic take
On complex matters. What they lack's the spur

To fresh discovery offered by the brake
On rapid processing that poets chose,
At least in part, for deeper insight's's sake,

Or that their skilled verse-rhythms might oppose
The rush to literal sense that gives no hold
For further thought. Such rapid reading knows

Well in advance what it's no doubt been told
To make of this or that Aesopian crux
By previous commentators, or some old

Authority beyond which point the buck's
Passed back as far as an invented *fons*
Et origo that stops the meaning-flux

By ruling that a master lexicon's
Our last, best guide in knowing where to draw
The line.
          'A fame that's longer-lived than bronze

Memorials' is the way our bards once saw
The kind of immortality they earned
By pure word-craftsmanship despite time's law

Of steady diminution in what's turned
To cultural account. Still it's the flip-
Side law I'd cite, the very one we spurned,

Us dialecticians, since it urged we slip
The bonds of purebred intellect and see
What texture, form and craftsmanship

In verse can do to rouse Calliope
Or sweeter-tongued Erato, and reveal
To willing ears and minds a language free

Of such constraints on utterance as we feel,
Us slaves of prosy custom, when impelled
To treat quotidian matters. Then we deal

With topics of the sort that should be spelled
Out clearly and without the needless swerve –
As it must seem – toward those senses held

In the vast tropological reserve
That poets, even versifiers like
Myself, may tap when some linguistic nerve

Is touched and metaphor is apt to strike
The mind with strange resemblance.
                    Yet why lurch
So far off revelation's path to hike

In regions where the intellect may search
For light beyond the variegated hues
Of this prismatic world, or form a church

For kindred spirits, when it's to the muse
Of poets *and* philosophers – our shared
Inspirer – that both parties should pay dues

For favours long received but not declared
By one of them. For this omission I
Must bear the blame in large part since I cared

Too greatly for the purity of my
Elect vocation, or its holding out
Against all taint of sense-infection by

Poetic speech, and not enough about
Those standing debts that we, the ones who plume
Ourselves on honest reckoning, dare to flout

By making every effort to assume
The role of sage and mentor. Thus we'd mock
The poets or those thinkers who found room

For tropes imported from the poets' stock
And turned to use for what we thought the mind-
Corrupting end of having listeners flock

To wonder at such words that left behind
All exercise of reason and provoked
In them unruly feelings of a kind

That threatened civil strife. Else the fire's stoked
By demagogues who share the poet's yen
For rousing passions alternately stroked

Into inert passivity and then
Whipped up into a frenzy by the skilled
Contrivances of those word-magic men,

The rhetoricians, whose desire to build
Their fake linguistic empires on the sand
Of mere persuasion leave that shabby guild

High on the list of junk professions banned
By the wise guardians of any state
Alert to such abuse.
                Yet now I stand

Before you honour-bound to propagate
A doctrine, or a way of life, that you'll
At first find more than hard to tolerate,

Thanks chiefly to your training in the School
Of Socrates, but later may regard
As your longed-for deliverance from the rule

Of sensory repression that debarred
Your minds from accessing the higher bliss
Of poetry and music. Just discard

The precepts that I've jettisoned in these,
My final thoughts, and you'll perhaps retrieve
What once was yours before old Socrates

Met you out walking, tugged you by the sleeve,
Suggested you debate some weighty theme
Of his shrewd choice, and got you to believe

Only such things as pass in academe
For knowledge or high wisdom. Let the word
Go out: not that I've given up my dream

Of reason as quite simply too absurd
For us to entertain, but more how I've
Come round to thinking that an idea heard

As poem or as music may revive
The soul to more immediate effect
Than any doctrine that would have us strive

To heed the edicts of pure intellect
And so resign such sensory delights
To their long history of willed neglect

At reason's hands.
                My friends, this theme invites
More music, or more poetry, but not –
For pity's sake – more chances to excite

The zeal for dialectic or allot
Yet further time to shop-talk of the same
Old sort, though now so slanted as to slot

In arguments that seek to shift the blame
From poetry to my fine-tuned techniques,
Back then, for mocking it. No cause for shame,

That perfect synthesis the poet seeks
Of soul conjoined to body's sensuous song,
Or body as the instrument that speaks

Soul's language, since it echoes like a gong
To chords resounding from the very heart
Of music's vibrant life. They both belong,

Philosopher and poet, quite apart
From the dull scholar or the humble scribe
Who spurn imagination's will to chart

Those regions unfrequented by the tribe
Of plain-prose sticklers lest they chance to hit
Some metaphoric trail or strike a vibe

That swiftly shatters their identikit
World-picture. So I leave you, friends as dear
To me as any, with the thought that it

Need not be just for last farewells that we're
Assembled now since maybe you'll have come,
No doubt reluctantly, to grasp how near-

Allied we are, the poet who by some
Inspired procedure, source to him unknown,
Speaks truth and we philosophers who plumb

Depths less opaque. Yet still we haunt the zone
Where poets were the first to dream those things
That we can't bring ourselves quite to condone

On intellectual grounds though our heart sings
At them and they provide the only gauge
Of truth for any thought of ours that springs

From any source beyond the concept-cage
Of thoughts already had by thinkers bred
Up to repeat them. Let's now turn the page

On that mind-locked condition and instead,
As poets do, entrust to metaphor's
Divine vouchsafing all that can't be said

Unless in words obedient to no laws
Save those adopted freely in the quest
For that which gives the 'ancient quarrel' pause

And thereby leaves both parties doubly blessed.

Showings (Wittgenstein): a double sestina

This inseparableness of everything in the world from language has intrigued modern thinkers, most notably Wittgenstein. If its limits—that is, the precise point at which sense becomes nonsense—could somehow be defined, then speakers would not attempt to express the inexpressible. Therefore, said Wittgenstein, do not put too great a burden upon language.

> Peter Farb,
> *Word-Play*

If a person tells me he has been to the worst places I have no reason to judge him; but if he tells me it was his superior wisdom that enabled him to go there, then I know he is a fraud.

> Ludwig Wittgenstein,
> *Personal Recollections* (ed. Rush Rhees)

The real discovery is the one that enables me to stop doing philosophy when I want to. The one that gives philosophy peace, so that it is no longer tormented by questions which bring itself into question.

> Wittgenstein,
> *Philosophical Investigations*

The world is everything that is the case.
All that's the case is all that we can say.
Some things cannot be said but may be shown.
These are the most important things in life.
A change in them will be a change of world.
Let silence show where saying leads astray.

So many ways we can be led astray!
Delinquent speech is not the only case,
Though certain evils may infect our world
Through word-abuse. Believing we can say
What matters most, in language or in life,
Is Russell's error. This much can be shown.

That's why my faithful few won't have it shown
How moral compass-points can swing astray
Even with such ascetic forms of life
Or utterance as mine. Count it a case
Of things-gone-wrong that nobody could say
Belonged exclusively to word or world.

Russell and Moore: they were my Cambridge world
Back then although, despite some kindness shown,
They failed to grasp how using words to say
Those things unsayable led sense astray.
Their verdict on me: genius, but a case
Of life screwed up by mind and mind by life.

'Just tell them that it's been a wonderful life.'
My dying words, and spoken from a world
So distant, now, from all that is the case
With their world that what's said by them, or shown,
Will likely lead my auditors astray
As much as anything I've had to say.

Yet there's some truth in what the others say,
My critics, who'd regard a tortured life
Like mine as leading and as led astray
Since formed within the solipsistic world
Of my obsessions. That's the sole thing shown,
They'd say, by such a cautionary case.

I keep my life a closed book just in case
Some rogue biographer should have his say
And seek, for no good cause, to have it shown
That there were certain chapters in that life
Kept secret from the academic world
Lest scandal lead my acolytes astray.

Yet could it be some young men went astray
Because I'd cruise the Prater and then case
The gay joints in my craving for a world
As far removed as possible from, say,

The wealth and privilege of my old life,
Or the mixed spite and condescension shown

By Moore and his Apostles? If I've shown
A seamy side, a will to go astray
In quest of what they'll call 'his other life',
It's not (the vulgar-Freudian view) a case
Of my abject desire that they should say
Harsh things that show me up before the world

For what I am. Rather, I deem that world
Of theirs a world in need of being shown
Such truths as neither they nor I can say
Since, in the saying, sense would go astray
And make me out a monster or a case
For some corrective treatment. It's my life,

Not anything I've written, but my life
As lived that bears sole witness to the world
Concerning just those matters in the case
Of Ludwig Wittgenstein that should be shown,
Not said, since uttering them sends words astray
And has them mimic what they fail to say.

And yet I ask: why think of 'show' and 'say'
In such bi-polar terms unless your life,
Like mine, has gone unspeakably astray
And left you stranded in an alien world
Where your 'condition' can at most be shown,
Not talked about or stated, just in case.

A modest claim: to say, not save, the world,
Yet still too statement-bound, as life has shown.
What was it went astray with what's the case?

No world exists that logothetes might say
'Here's all we've shown: that words bring worlds to life'.
What if 'the case' *just is* what goes astray?

Problems of Philosophy (Russell)

*Three passions, simple but overwhelmingly strong, have governed
my life: the longing for love, the search for knowledge, and unbear-
able pity for the suffering of mankind. These passions, like great
winds, have blown me hither and thither, in a wayward course,
over a deep ocean of anguish, reaching to the very verge of despair.*

The Autobiography of Bertrand Russell

*I resolved from the beginning of my quest that I would not be
misled by sentiment and desire into beliefs for which there was no
good evidence.*

Bertrand Russell,
Fact and Fiction

No impulse undeformed by intellect.
The pity is that pity's without end.
How cure my old thought-feeling disconnect?

The aesthetes say: 'just feel, just introspect,
Don't reach for some grand theory to defend'.
No impulse undeformed by intellect.

The thinkers say: 'trust reason to correct
Those sentiments that Bloomsbury-ward might tend'.
How cure my old thought-feeling disconnect?

No doubt it's needs of mine that I project
Along with each new doctrine I commend:
No impulse undeformed by intellect.

Yet this I know: if pity runs unchecked
It yields no wise or healing dividend.
How cure my old thought-feeling disconnect?

Time was when they were coupled up direct,
Says Eliot, till some discord spiked the blend:
No impulse undeformed by intellect.

The fault's one any watcher might detect
Who saw how I betrayed them, friend with friend.
How cure my old thought-feeling disconnect?

Can't really blame it on the Bloomsbury sect
Although their class act helped to set the trend.
No impulse undeformed by intellect.

Too many, those relationships I wrecked;
No kindlier light, no saving grace to lend.
How cure my old thought-feeling disconnect?

Moore made things simpler, as you might expect.
'Beauty and love: on these our lives depend.'
No impulse undeformed by intellect.

'Let those ideals your every thought inflect',
He said, 'and their high truth you'll comprehend.'
How cure my old thought-feeling disconnect?

God knows the aim's not one that I'd reject,
Though suiting those with leisure-time to spend.
No impulse undeformed by intellect.

For my type, the best hope's to decathect
By further thought those thoughts we can't transcend.
How cure my old thought-feeling disconnect?
No impulse undeformed by intellect.

Time and the Physicist

The uniform nature of time is scarcely the only feature where our intuition has turned out to be mistaken. To everybody's surprise, the difference between past and future fails to show up in the elementary equations that govern the physical world. But the discovery that has been the most disconcerting of all has been finding out that the notion of 'present' does not make sense in the larger universe; it only makes sense in the vicinity of us slow human critters.

Carlo Rovelli

We common readers continue to look up to them [physicists] as the repository of knowledge and begin to regard them as the custodians of the spiritual element in the universe. They – or to speak more moderately, some of them – have long aspired to the mantle of the prophets; now we thrust the mantle upon them . . . The situation does not lack an element of comedy.

L. Susan Stebbing

One way of looking at it: time's the rate
Of outcomes fixed, doubts laid to rest,
Hypotheses shown true
Or falsified,
And all our clue-by-clue
Inductive reasonings put to test
As more conjectures pass their use-by date,
Lives work out pretty much as guessed
(Or not), and things that do,
Or did, betide
Us right out of the blue
Turn past-event and join the rest
Of what we once put down to chance or fate.

Rovelli says we get it wrong: we think,
Like Newton, time's a one-way flow
Past-present-future, or
Espouse the line
That time's the very core
Of human being, what we know
Most intimately in ourselves, yet blink
At any thought that we should go
Some abstract way to draw
Its superfine
Gradations out, ignore
What Bergson said, and strive to show
How well clock-time and inner time-scales sync.

Rovelli's view of time: its arrow's sped
Along by entropy, by all
The multitude of ways
The Second Law
(Thermodynamics) says
No going back, no second call,
And no prognosticating what's ahead
Except the physicist's long-haul
Heat-death-based bid to faze
The hopers, awe
Post-humanists, and raise
The culture-stock of those in thrall
To any doomsday script with science-cred.

Old news: like Eddington, he's out to stun
A readership once prone to kid
Themselves they'd got time right
Despite their lack
Of physics-grasp. This might,
With help from pop-sci primers, rid
The world of sundry errors like the one
About time passing, lift the lid
On all the recondite
Events they track,

Those physicists, and fight
The vulgar prejudice that hid
A realm where writs of common sense don't run.

Fair point: we've science-ignorance to blame
For much that's wrong, not least the sorts
Of falsehood pushed by those
With most to gain
If we're led by the nose
And swallow science-lite reports
Produced, to wide political acclaim,
By some committee that distorts
All findings apt to pose
A threat or strain
Our willingness to close
Eyes, ears, or bias-checking thoughts
To what goes on in that mock-science game.

Yet should the latest, physics-based ideas
Of time and space get so far out
Of kilter with the way
They seem to us
Then, really, who's to say
It's our ideas we're bound to doubt
Instead, more sensibly, of thinking: here's
An instance where the most devout
Scientophile might lay
Old ghosts and thus
Come to accept there may
Be truths that lack such physics-clout
Yet hold for us across these new frontiers.

Skip eight decades and maybe you'll conclude
That Stebbing got it right, or that
The jury's out, or – if
You find the whole
Thing pointless – that their tiff,
Stebbing *v* Eddington, was flat-

Out misconceived, its terms too plainly skewed
To mean what each was aiming at,
For Stebbing a nice riff
On her chief role
In roping off the cliff
Where science-lemmings splat,
For Eddington a lesson to the brood
Of physics-phobes who'd got off pat,
Like her, a way to sniff
At the high toll
Of good sense on a whiff
Of scientism. All old hat,
Rovelli thinks, that routine attitude

Of undisguised hostility between
Two cultures that, in truth, should rub
Along just fine since they're
Not out to seize
The high ground but to share
It on his terms: physics the nub
Of every quest for knowledge, every keen
New aspirant to join the club
Of science, but – with care
To quell unease
In those who must forswear
Such things – 'the arts' as fit to scrub
Up their antique credentials and so glean
The kindly credit due to sub-
Altern endeavors where
The legatees
Of everyman find their
Back-hand remittance for the snub
Renewed when Science PR sets the scene.

Six Villanelles on Quantum Themes

1) Ultraviolet

The amount of radiation emitted in a given frequency range should be proportional to the number of modes in that range. The best of classical physics suggested that all modes had an equal chance of being produced, and that the number of modes went up proportionally to the square of the frequency. But the predicted continual increase in radiated energy with frequency (dubbed the 'ultraviolet catastrophe') did not happen. Nature knew better.

Hyperphysics

Things can't go on like this, you must agree.
Unless the scale proves discrete it's a case
Of ultraviolet catastrophe.

Good news: the black box comes with guarantee
That things change stepwise, limits stay in place.
We can't go on like this, you must agree.

It's quantum physics that provides the key;
Discreteness rules so we'll not have to face
Some ultraviolet catastrophe.

Start infra-red, shift wavelengths, then we'll see
Just how we fare as things heat up apace:
They can't go on like this, you must agree.

Discrete or not, discretion bids that we
Grow warmer step by step lest it take place,
That ultraviolet catastrophe.

That's why, despite Planck's limit-point decree,
The comfort's one we're hard-put to embrace.
Things can't go on like this, you must agree;
Fear ultraviolet catastrophe!

2) The Copenhagen View

Bohr: 'Heisenberg, I have to say – if people are to be measured strictly in terms of observable quantities. . . .'

Heisenberg: 'Then we should need a strange new quantum ethics.'

Bohr: You've never been able to understand the suggestiveness of paradox and contradiction. That's your problem. You live and breathe paradox and contradiction, but you can no more see the beauty of them than the fish can see the beauty of the water.

Michael Frayn,
Copenhagen

The Copenhagen view: take both on board,
Wave/particle; let contradiction thrive!
It's logic's either/or we can't afford.

Both/and brings hope of harmony restored
So our twin paradigms may co-survive.
The Copenhagen view: take both on board.

Let those logicians henceforth be ignored
When for strict bivalence they vainly strive:
It's logic's either/or we can't afford.

Else their demand would have us lovers floored,
Along with half the physicists alive!
The Copenhagen view: take both on board.

So long as all appearances accord
With our best theory, give it a high five!
It's logic's either/or we can't afford.

Why emulate those realists who deplored
Our line till their pet theories took a dive?
The Copenhagen view: take both on board.

Then logic's apt to seem a mouse that roared
And pipe down once anomalies arrive.
It's logic's either/or we can't afford.

Yet still they tell us 'truth's its own reward'
And say it's with unreason we connive:
The Copenhagen view: take both on board.

Could be it's why their case strikes such a chord
With us who'd some good middle way contrive.
It's logic's either/or we can't afford

To recognise, but there's a touch of fraud
About the consolations we derive.
The Copenhagen view: take both on board.

Let's face it, these are cat-box thoughts we've shored
Against truth's quantum-state-reducing drive.
It's logic's either/or we can't afford.
The Copenhagen view: take both on board.

3) Hidden Variables

> *It can be argued that in trying to see behind the formal predictions of quantum theory we are just making trouble for ourselves. Was not precisely this the lesson that had to be learned before quantum mechanics could be constructed, that it is futile to try to see behind the observed phenomena?*
>
> *Theoretical physicists live in a classical world, looking out into a quantum-mechanical world. The latter we describe only subjectively, in terms of procedures and results in our classical domain.*
>
> J.S. Bell,
> *Speakable and Unspeakable in Quantum Mechanics*

'No hidden variables', the rule-book goes.
They'd take the weirdness out and set things straight.
Why the equations work nobody knows.

No in-the-source spin-values to disclose:
They'd fix beforehand every change of state.
'No hidden variables', the rule-book goes.

Those realist-friendly theories fail to pose
Such questions as our mystic times dictate.
Why the equations work nobody knows.

New-agers jump at anything that throws
A spanner in the works; at any rate
'No hidden variables', the rule-book goes.

It's any realist questioning of those
Remote entangled particles they hate.
Why the equations work nobody knows.

Again, the fear's not hard to diagnose:
Love works so long as it stays part blind-date.
'No hidden variables', the rule-book goes.

Or rather: as the intimacy grows
So must our light-year distances dilate.
Why the equations work nobody knows.

Maybe that's why Bohr/Heisenberg first chose
This way-out view of things to propagate:
'No hidden variables', the rule-book goes.

Quantum entanglement: the ratios
Mean we're in touch though messages must wait.
Why the equations work nobody knows,

But then, why worry? All the data shows
They come out right where values commutate.
'No hidden variables', the rule-book goes.

Though Einstein kept the Bohr crowd on their toes
With thought-experiments, they'd just re-state
'Why the equations work nobody knows'.

And us, let's not forget what closeness owes
To distance and not share in Echo's fate.
'No hidden variables', the rule-book goes;
Why the equations work nobody knows.

4) Decoherence

> *. . . . the nonevent in question is due to a 'Quantum Oblivion' effect, where a very brief virtual interaction undergoes 'unhappening'. Oblivion underlies quantum erasure and several other peculiar effects. [Some have proposed] a retrocausal evolution that accounts for such self-cancellation, involving exchange of negative physical values between earlier and later events.*
>
> Elitzur, Cohen and Shushi,
> 'The Too-Late-Choice Experiment'

No point our asking how it ended here.
Wave-functions cancel; antecedents fade.
It's our twinned histories that disappear.

Some word, some gesture came to interfere
And so produced an outcome long delayed:
No point our asking how it ended here.

First irony: though things now show up clear
The past turns secretive, anterograde.
It's our twinned histories that disappear.

And second: why then presuppose that we're
The 'we' that launched this temporal glissade?
No point our asking how it ended here.

This eigenstate's our only souvenir
Of states once superposed but now decayed.
It's our twinned histories that disappear.

Bit wasted, all that swish measurement gear,
With outcomes macroscopically displayed;
No point our asking how it ended here.

Says Feynman: it's when path-integrals smear
That order quells the quantum-state cascade.
It's our twinned histories that disappear.

Says Bohm: allow a pilot-wave to steer
The particle and then you've got it made.
Still no point asking how it ended here.

Says Bohr: agreed, this quantum stuff is queer,
But that's how the new physics game is played.
It's our twinned histories that disappear.

I say: small solace from the quantum-sphere
For us old lags who've looked to it for aid.
No point our asking how it ended here;
It's our twinned histories that disappear.

5) *Many Worlds*

> *The Many-Worlds Interpretation of quantum mechanics holds that
> there are many worlds which exist in parallel at the same space and
> time as our own. The existence of the other worlds makes it pos-
> sible to remove randomness and action at a distance from quantum
> theory and thus from all physics.*

> Lev Vaidman

The access problem, but let's not despair.
Let's give that Many-Worlds idea a shot.
Things might go otherwise in worlds elsewhere.

We like to dream them up in our armchair
Though robust types insist we'd better not.
The access problem, but let's not despair.

Though wave-collapse precludes our being there
It lets our counterfactuals hit the spot:
Things might go otherwise in worlds elsewhere.

Why rule them out if life gets hard to bear
And they're the only Shangri-Las you've got?
The access problem, but let's not despair.

Why not hypothesise another pair
Like us, our doubles in an upbeat plot?
Things might go otherwise in worlds elsewhere.

Still we and they, our counterparts, could share
No trans-world intimations of what's what:
The access problem, but let's not despair.

Some make-believe such happenings are rare
Though possible, but they're the pop-sci lot.
Things might go otherwise in worlds elsewhere.

It's that word 'might' that's set the hoper's snare
Since wavicles first passed the double slot:
The access problem, but let's not despair.

'We bring no this-world answer to your prayer',
The experts say, 'no means to tie the knot:
Things might go otherwise in worlds elsewhere'.

Still hold-out hopers may elect to err
Since they've no expert's copy-book to blot.
The access problem, but let's not despair;
Things might go otherwise in worlds elsewhere.

6) Many Minds

The Many Minds interpretation examines the consequences of the Everett Many-Worlds interpretation from the perspective of the mind. Rather than many worlds branching at each quantum decision point, it is the observer's mind that is branching.

Yoav Aviram

Let's see if Many Minds can do the trick.
It's Many Worlds plus minds to sift and sort.
Just one wave-function, so we two might click.

Those other quantum theories (take your pick)
All have their points but finally fall short:
Let's see if Many Minds can do the trick.

It says: if those world-versions seem to flick
Past endlessly, let's put it down to thought.
Just one wave-function, so we two might click.

It uses all the same arithmetic
And all same equations we've been taught:
Let's see if Many Minds can do the trick.

The difference is, this theory doesn't stick
At disjunct worlds where mind-states go for naught:
Just one wave-function, so we two might click.

It counts them both within its bailiwick
Since minds decide for worlds: launch or abort!
Let's see if Many Minds can do the trick.

Then maybe us two loners, if we're quick,
Might co-perceive a world of first resort.
Just one wave-function, so we two might click;
Let's see if Many Worlds can do the trick.

Kant: border-crossing (sestinas)

I had to deny knowledge in order to make room for faith.

Human reason has this peculiar fate that in one species of its knowledge it is burdened by questions which, as prescribed by the very nature of reason itself, it is not able to ignore, but which, as transcending all its powers, it is also not able to answer.

The light dove, cleaving the air in her free flight, and feeling its resistance, might imagine that its flight would be still easier in empty space.

Immanuel Kant,
Critique of Pure Reason

The whole analytic of aesthetic judgment forever assumes that one can distinguish rigorously between the intrinsic and the extrinsic . . . . Deconstruction must neither reframe nor dream of the pure absence of the frame. These two apparently contradictory gestures are the very ones – and they are systematically indissociable – of what is here deconstructed.

Jacques Derrida,
'Parergon', in *The Truth in Painting*

I

My watchword: let all thought observe due bounds.
Curb reason's flight; set knowledge on firm ground;
Restrict its scope, and so make room for faith.
Let faith not claim to know but rather think
Those postulates of reason that good will
May raise into a true kingdom of ends.

Not that each starts just where the other ends.
No such dogmatic beating of the bounds,
But a critique that shows us how they will

Keep hopping borders, filching bits of ground,
Or annexing new land just when you think
They've signed up to the system in good faith.

I meant it when I said 'It's here, in faith,
That my whole enterprise begins and ends'.
Yet those there are who still prefer to think
That a religion broached 'within the bounds
Of reason only' must yield vital ground
For atheists to colonise at will.

Not so, say I: those God-proofs surely will,
Once proven false, leave no resort for faith
Since their ill-judged incursions on its ground
Mix up conceptual means with rational ends
And so create, within pure reason's bounds,
Such strife as harms our very power to think.

Yet, strangely, thoughts like these are what we think,
Us wayward types, each time the errant will
To venture out beyond such prudent bounds
Asserts itself and bids us pin our faith
Once more to certain speculative ends
That have us soar too far from solid ground.

Yet when I'd run the last of them to ground,
Those vexed antinomies, I came to think
That all productive thought begins and ends
With speculative impasse, so my will
To rein in contradictions shows less faith
In reason than the soarer's leaps and bounds.

Why then yield ground to his insensate will?
They err who think to fly on wings of faith.
My groundwork ends where thought exceeds all bounds.

II

My second rule: for everything its frame!
Let intuitions be a perfect fit
For concepts; let each moral problem-case
Be brought beneath the universal rule
Of moral law; let beauty likewise lie
Within the frame of judgment fixed by taste.

In each case judgment would come down to taste,
And taste alone, if thought supplied no frame
By which to know just where the limits lie
Between art and non-art, or persons fit
To judge and those unfit, or how the rule
May brook exception in the special case

Of genius. Yet this has to be the case
With moral judgments also, where a taste
For problems, quandaries, dilemmas, rule-
Book upsets, and their like may crack the frame
Or serve to show that what makes judgment fit
That case cannot be how the ground-rules lie.

My book says: always wrong to tell a lie.
Why so? It constitutes a clear-cut case
Of setting other persons up as fit
Means to some end that, through our vicious taste
For self-advantage, leads us to re-frame
Their personhood as ours to over-rule.

Yet how uphold this universal rule
That ends trump means as reason not to lie
Against the counter-arguments they frame,
My critics, when they cite some awkward case
(For me, that is, though wholly to their taste)
Where my truth-telling maxim doesn't fit?

Instance: the blood-crazed axeman throws a fit
At your front door, screams 'Is X here?', and rule
'Speak-True!' instructs: 'Let not your strong distaste
For bloodshed tell you it's OK to lie –
At least a lesser wrong – if that's the case',
Or any such scenario you might frame.

And if it's fit and proper, then, to lie
And break my rule, then I'll admit this case
Gives me a taste of things no law can frame.

III

I once said: three great questions make me think.
They are: 'What can I know?', 'What should I do?',
And then 'What might I reasonably hope?'.
All three drew negatives. That which we know
Can have at most such warrant as belongs
To those who track its limits as they ought.

Please note: this epistemic sense of 'ought'
Applies lest we rash over-reachers think
We've somehow come to grasp that which belongs
Beyond our mortal ken. My point: make do
With those innate resources that we know
Can offer human knowers their best hope

Of cognitive advance. Shun the false hope
That has us striving to cognise what ought,
By rights, to find no place for claims to know
Since given us as ideas fit to think
In speculative mode, as those may do
To whom the dove's sky-cleaving gift belongs.

Yet it's that yen of mine for what belongs –
What goes with what, how knowledge, morals, hope
Stand vis-à-vis each other as they do –
It's that compulsion that perhaps I ought

To strive against, the more so when I think
That strains are showing up in ways I know

From past thought-venturing. For if 'to know'
Is, properly, a factive that belongs
To things known truly, not just things we think,
Then I know for a truth that my one hope
Of finally connecting 'is' and 'ought'
Is to cease splitting things up as I do

And take my turn at lumping. This might do
All that I've dreamed of doing: have us know
Where hopes are rational, fill out the 'ought'
With moral substance, then say what belongs
To what in such a way that knowledge, hope
And virtue join as plain good sense would think.

Yet it won't do, this mind-trick that belongs
To sanguine sorts who 'know' they've grounds for hope
And for whom 'ought' translates 'do as I think'.

Reflections from Rancière

A man cannot search either for what he knows or for what he does not know. He cannot search for what he knows – since he knows it, there is no need to search – nor for what he does not know, for he does not know what to look for.

Plato,
Meno

The master always keeps a piece of learning – that is to say, a piece of the student's ignorance – up his sleeve. I understood that, says the satisfied student. You think so, corrects the master. In fact, there's a difficulty here that I've been sparing you until now. We will explain it when we get to the corresponding lesson. What does this mean? asks the curious student. I could tell you, responds the master, but it would be premature: you wouldn't understand at all. It will be explained to you next year . . . . Thus does the triumphant Achilles drag Hector's corpse, attached to his chariot, around the city of Troy.

Jacques Rancière
The Ignorant Schoolmaster: five lessons in intellectual emancipation

1

It's Meno's paradox I take to heart.
You taught me this yet proved your teaching vain.
If naught's foreknown how then can learning start?

It seems those plus-marks on my progress-chart
Were things that I forgot, then learned again.
It's Meno's paradox I take to heart.

Forgetting's a much underrated art,
Said Nietzsche, one acquired to keep us sane.
If all's foreknown how then can learning start?

Well-known to you but not to poor Descartes
Who thought all truths must show up sharp and plain.
It's Meno's paradox I take to heart.

You taught me: no thought-strategy so smart
It yields up truths fresh-minted in the brain.
If naught's foreknown how then can learning start?

That's how my anamnesis plays its part
By setting your maieutic skills in train.
It's Meno's paradox I take to heart;
If all's foreknown how then can learning start?

2

Let's see that neither of us takes the lead.
Such pedagogy begs a modest air.
The *Meno* ploy's much likelier to succeed.

The ignorant schoolmaster finds his creed
In this shrewd maxim of Jacques Rancière:
Let's see that neither of us takes the lead.

The old-style pedagogues still say 'Force-feed
The ignorami', but those dotards err:
The *Meno* ploy's much likelier to succeed.

It says we'll both get more by heart once freed
From that old itch to hog the teacher's share.
Let's see that neither of us takes the lead.

It's classroom inequalities that breed
The teacher's rage and pupil's vengeful prayer:
The *Meno* ploy's much likelier to succeed.

Else they'd have recognised the mutual need
For ignorance between that mind-locked pair.
Let's see that neither of us takes the lead;
The *Meno* ploy's much likelier to succeed.

3

Unwise to think you're holding all the keys.
That way, you'll find they've jammed the lock and fled.
Make your best guide the *eiron* Socrates.

His wager was he'd lead them, by degrees,
To think 'No telling lead from being led'.
Unwise to think you're holding all the keys.

His way, I guess, you'll not do much to please
The ruling class (think hemlock!), but instead
Make your best guide the *eiron* Socrates.

Then it's both parties feel the tightened squeeze
Of an elenchus, yet still think ahead:
Unwise to think you're holding all the keys.

Old pedagogues would have you on your knees,
Not thinking inch-by-inch along the thread.
Make your best guide the *eiron* Socrates.

The end's what neither party yet foresees,
Since each has no fixed aim to take as read.
Unwise to think you're holding all the keys;
Make your best guide the *eiron* Socrates.

4

Wise ignorance but not the holy fool.
Let folly not be praised for heaven's sake.
No yield from nescience except in school.

'Seek truths unthought-of' is the only rule.
Think dialectically where they're at stake.
Wise ignorance but not the holy fool.

Just ignorant full-stop, the teacher who'll
Tell pupils to enjoy a thinking-break:
No yield from nescience except in school.

Don't let Erasmus trick you: ridicule,
Not praise, should greet each sainted folly-fake.
Wise ignorance but not the holy fool.

He's much too single-track: thinking's a dual-
Drive vehicle so think which routes to take;
No yield from nescience except in school.

The ignorant schoolmaster reckons you'll
Exceed all grade-predictions he could make.
Wise ignorance but not the holy fool;
No yield from nescience except in school.

5

His axiom: equal shares in mother-wit.
If things seem otherwise, you just ask why,
Then equalise to make the axiom fit.

Corollary: should circumstance permit,
Low-flying types would touch a common sky.
His axiom: equal shares in mother-wit.

Old pedagogues have arguments to pit
Against him, but he runs the same reply:
'Then equalise to make the axiom fit'.

It just means trading in your teacher's kit
For one that does without the clever guy.
His axiom: equal shares in mother-wit.

Perhaps by this we'll do our modest bit
To give the Rancière theory a good try,
Then equalise to make the axiom fit.

Good chance us twin co-acolytes may quit
School finally with equal space to fly.
His axiom: equal shares in mother-wit;
Then equalise to make the axiom fit.

An Uncommon Reader

It is not expected of critics that they should help us to make sense of our lives; they are bound only to attempt the lesser feat of making sense of the ways we try to make sense of our lives.

At some very low level, we all share certain fictions about time, and they testify to the continuity of what is called human nature, however conscious some, as against others, may become of the fictive quality of these fictions.

This is an age of theory, and theory is both difficult and usually not related to anything that meets the wider interest I speak of.

Frank Kermode

They ask me 'Why no novels, why not try
Your hand at fiction; surely you could use
All those ideas, those insights, all the rare
And subtle arts that were your specialty

As literary critic and apply
The self-same gifts to any theme you choose,
Creating narratives that might compare
With the all the fictive texts you've helped us see

In new and complex ways?'. They flatter my
Poor efforts in that line, my quest for clues
As to what constitutes the reader's share
In finding some interpretative key

That unlocks secrets and what just might lie
More squarely with the author's canny ruse
For bringing us to recognize how they're
In charge of every hermeneutic spree

That otherwise risks sending sense awry
And all too easily forgetting whose
The mind that shapes the tale. A certain flair

For posing suchlike questions, a degree

Of theory-primed intentness to defy
The academic norms, to spread the news
From France (although the scoffer's phrase 'armchair
Rebellion' comes to mind) – these seem to me

The only gifts, if such they are, that I
Would think to bring in tribute to the muse,
If such she is, of us poor hacks who dare
Profess the critic's trade. Still there's a plea

Worth entering, one that lacks the note of high
Arnoldian zeal whose dwindling residues
Still haunt the dreaming spires but may yet bear,
Once cleared of pious cant, some scrutiny,

If just 'the passing tribute of a sigh'
From Arnold's fretful heirs. In truth we lose
No more than he lost, self-condemned to wear
The patched and faded robes of prophecy,

The togs of a Romantic age gone by
When poets blazed and the Victorian blues,
That torment of belatedness and prayer
For hope renewed, had not yet come to be

The music of the times. What cause to cry
'Born late!' in any wilderness with views
To cherish all around? I'd rather err
On the bright side and recommend that we

Lit-crit trained Jeremiahs pipe our eye
Less readily and see we don't confuse
Short-term effects for long-term or declare
The outlook hopeless. With a moiety

Of clerkly scepticism we may ply

The ancient trade of critics and peruse
Dark texts for passages that square
With no set protocol, no abc

Of reading. That might serve as alibi
For skimmers chiefly anxious to excuse
Their preference for idling in dead air
While, scarcely felt by them, the energy

Of clashing signifiers rends the sky
For readers less in hock to the taboos
Enforced by taste or custom. Doctrinaire
Post-structuralists may celebrate the 'free-

Play of the signifier', but they'd fly
More scenically if they'd just opt to cruise
Once in a while, with altitude to spare,
Or (not to milk my metaphor) just see

What's lost by theories dead-set to deny
The yield that comes of paying equal dues,
Ideally, to the giddy joys of their
Utopian devising and the pre-

Post-structuralist way of sometimes getting by
On plot and character. Each will accuse
The other of displaying too much care
For their pet notions, reading sloppily,

Treating the novelist as their fall-guy,
Or waiting for a chance to put the screws
On rival critics. Call it savoir-faire,
Having it both ways, fake humility,

Or (my strong preference) having fish to fry
With both lots, 'common readers' and the crews
Of theory's Fleet Air Arm. I've tried to pair
Them off by seeing points where they agree,

Like favoring those novels that untie
Their plot-knots gradually, that hide the ruse
Behind their fictive workings, or prepare
Its revelation through an artistry

That still has things to hide. Such fighting-shy
Of bluntness, such reluctance to enthuse
Where caution's called for, such a host of scare-
Quotes gently pleading 'Don't take it from me!',

And such a courteous – or is it sly? –
Reminder that these subtleties bemuse
The recent holder of a Cambridge chair
In English Literature (short-term i.d.,

Not a good time) just as they mystify
The reader who, quite sensibly, eschews
All ventures into alien country where
High theory rules. The papers note with glee

This irony that has the alumni
Of Oxbridge lined up ready to abuse
'Those theorists', me included, though I'd share
That label sooner than the company

Of bonehead scholar-toffs. That's maybe why
You'll find me writing essay-length reviews
For a 'broad' readership, and not the fare
Served up to members of the clerisy,

Like me back then, in articles well-nigh
Incomprehensible to readers whose
Life-interests didn't run that way. It's there,
With 'mankind in the middest', that the key

Must lie, the guiding light to us who pry,
Discreetly, for some episode that skews
The story-line or lays a textual snare
Arcane enough to snag the devotee

Of theory yet with twists enough to vie
With thrillers or crime novels. Let us schmooze
Once in a while, pen causeries, repair
The high/low culture rift, or referee

The match so both contenders can descry,
In no man's land, what either might construe
As novel-reading's good *vin ordinaire*
Yet with a touch of theory's *bel esprit*.

Ten Limericks after Kurt Gödel

*I wish to designate the following as the most important question
which can be asked with regard to the axioms: to prove that they are
not contradictory, that a definite number of logical steps based upon
them can never lead to contradictory results.*

David Hilbert

*Any consistent formal system F within which a certain amount of
elementary arithmetic can be carried out is incomplete; i.e., there
are statements of the language of F that can neither be proved nor
disproved in F.*

Panu Raatikainen,
'Gödel's Incompleteness Theorems'

*For in reality Cantor's conjecture must be either true or false, and
its undecidability from the axioms as known today can only mean
that these axioms do not contain a complete description of reality.*

Kurt Gödel

The mathematician Kurt Gödel
Found a proof that made colleagues' blood curdle,
For it left them in shock
When he proved you could knock
A big hole in all proofs - quite a hurdle!

That his theorem held good all the same
Brought a shift in the rules of the game
Since reliance on formal
Procedures as normal
Showed you stuck in that Banksy-like frame.

That some axioms can't be decided
True/false was a thought that collided
With the cardinal rule
That they'd learned back in school
And by which they routinely abided.

So it was that they'd once bet their shirts
On the checklist of Hilbert dead-certs
Which they thought would soon yield
Every prize in the field
But now reeled at this stunner of Kurt's.

For it's tough luck (what luck could be tougher?)
If your thought-train runs into the buffer
So it's quickly derailed
And your paper's marked 'failed':
Such a blow for high-hopers to suffer!

Follow Wittgenstein, dump Bertrand Russell,
Or you'll find all this logical fuss'll
Just get in the way
Of what plain words can say
Without flexing an analyst's muscle.

Still it died hard, the logicist dream
Of a bivalent truth-value scheme
Where a gap in your proof
Meant you'd managed to goof,
Not subvert the whole logic-regime.

As for Gödel, he chose to construe it
As a proof we could grasp or intuit
By some power of the mind
Wholly different in kind
From the way that rule-followers do it.

Thus he thought we'd do better to seek
Fresh assurance in Plato's mystique
Of a transcendent realm
Where, with *nous* at the helm,
They could steer ourselves down Problem Creek.

Yet it must be cold comfort for those
Still appalled at the spanner it throws
Into every last hope
To explore the full scope
Of what logic alone might disclose.

Note

'Banksy-like frame': a reference to the British street-artist's instantly famous self-destroying/self-consuming work 'Girl with a Balloon'. This stencil auto-shredded as it was being auctioned at Sotheby's for just over £1 million. It was subsequently re-titled 'Love In a Bin'.

Darwin's Dog

My dog . . . was lying on the lawn during a hot and still day; but at a little distance a slight breeze occasionally moved an open parasol, which would have been wholly disregarded by the dog, had any one stood near it. As it was, every time that the parasol slightly moved, the dog growled fiercely and barked. He must, I think, have reasoned to himself, in a rapid and unconscious manner, that movement without any apparent cause indicated the presence of some strange living agent, and no stranger had a right to be on his territory.

Charles Darwin,
The Descent of Man

When you call a man a dog with obscure praise, or treat a dog as half-human, you do not much believe in the Fall of Man, you assume a rationalist view of man as the most triumphant of the animals . . . . 'Dog', it is absurd but half-true to say, became to the eighteenth-century sceptic what God had been to his ancestors, the last security behind human values.

William Empson,
The Structure of Complex Words

I

There's some things I don't say for Emma's sake.
She has her Christian faith, a simple creed.
The parasol moves slightly in the breeze.
The dog stirs, sniffs some presence in the air.

From God to dog: a journey hard to make,
And one that ends far short of Emma's need,
Yet travelled now, I find, with perfect ease
As dog-communing takes the place of prayer.

Dear Emma fears these thoughts of mine will shake
Her faith, bring back old doubts and fears that she'd
Once bring to me in hopes I might appease
Them with consoling words we two could share.

Me too, if truth be known; I've my own stake
In her distress, those tears of hers that plead
Some respite from the age's long disease,
That loss so dimly felt yet hard to bear.

Still there are joys that salve the spirit's ache,
Like having dogs of amiable breed,
Like mine, who don't just have a trick to please
Their so-called masters, or possess a flair

For imitation, but at times partake
So deeply of our thoughts and moods that we'd
Be doltish to deny the indices
Of species-bonding manifested there.

You'll tell me his beguiling traits are fake,
Put on for food or play, but should indeed
That sometimes be the case, then think what these
Sly homo saps will do in quest of their

Objectives, high or low. Often opaque
To us, another's feelings, though I read
My dog's, he mine, with all the expertise
Of tacit knowledge and a kinship rare

In quality yet known to those who'd break
With doctrines that require we pay no heed
To our late-dawning cognisance that he's
No mere automaton, that creature there.

Then, rid of such thought-hobblers, we might wake
To modes of creature-being that exceed
Man's lonely eminence, set up to squeeze
The beast back into its primeval lair.

II

Ah yes, the parasol! It slipped my mind,
What with all these diversions on the theme
Of man and dog. My point: he felt or saw,
Through half-closed eyes, the breeze begin to sway

The parasol, which naturally inclined
My dog to think – by dint of what would seem
Straightforward inductive reasoning from the law
Of push and pull – that it behaved that way

Due solely to some willed intent behind
The push. So souls are summoned to redeem
The zombie flesh, or spirit to restore
The waning self, or here a *dieu caché*

To stir the parasol, as men assigned
A host of tutelary gods to beam
Or frown on their endeavors, till the more
Astute or tidy-minded came to say

'One God and one God only'. For they'd find
Him suited to their purpose, this supreme
Disposer who'd dire punishments in store
For those who dared to disbelieve what they,

His chosen few, infallibly divined
As God's own will. Picked for the rival team
Were all who saw their way clear to explore
Our ties to nature with its whole array

Of life-forms and reject the Bible-bind
That says mankind alone should gain esteem
In His eyes. Me, I favor a ground-floor
Approach that works up from the mortal clay

We share with every branch of creature-kind
And shows how that anthropocentric scheme,

Though God-decreed, must willfully ignore
The myriad signs and tokens that betray

Our species ancestry. It's still entwined
With theirs at every point, witness the gleam
In that dog's eyes when I move to the door
At walk-time, or preempt his wish to play

Some favorite game, or know from our combined
Intuiting what kind of waking dream
Might prompt those growls and whimpers that can draw
Forth feelings deep as any words convey.

III

That 'god' reversed spells 'dog' is something I'd
Not say to Emma, though it seems to me,
Absurdly, just the sort of odd surprise
That language springs on us when change of heart

And mind is in the offing, or the tide
Of thought is on the turn so words are free
To take wing in the quest for distant skies
And lands far off the cautious sailor's chart.

An age of doubt is what it signified,
A dwindling faith in God as referee
For any rank-disputes that might arise
On the Great Chain of Being, and a start

Toward finding ways across the great divide
Twixt man and beast. Faith once required that we,
Bruised apples of God's eye, not recognize
How close the creature-bond, how wrong Descartes

With his implacable desire to hide
All evidence that might provide a key
To how they first arose, those natural ties
Whose claim on us no doctrine can outsmart

Since felt afresh each time we cast aside
Faith's stubborn edict. Then at last we'll see
What's within view whenever we surmise
That there's far less sets man and dog apart

Than lets both creatures join to over-ride
Such differences. It's that propinquity
In mode of being that alone supplies
Our own and their past mastery in the art

Of wordlessly perceiving what's implied
By gesture, tone of voice, and all that he,
My dog, negotiates through ears and eyes
Alert to every cue and primed to dart

Off momently in search of some untried
Sense-channel. I ask Emma: can it be
Such blasphemy to think we empathize
In ways unknown where head dictates to heart?

IV

It's the great apes, not dogs, who mostly gain
Star treatment among naturalists like my
Grandfather, old Erasmus, who've long guessed
The truth of evolution but who chose,

No doubt on grounds of prudence, to refrain
From intimating certain things that I
Was better placed to say since now possessed
Of facts and findings quite unknown to those

Great pioneers. Ape-watchers now take brain-
Size, finger-toe arithmetic, or high
Performance in some puzzle-solving test
To be the kind of evidence that goes

To prove that we've inherited a strain
Of whatsoever went to qualify
The great apes as the animals most blest
With proto-human attributes. This shows

How apt they are, those thinkers, to ordain
The thought-procedures they themselves apply
As more innately 'human' than the rest
Of our distinctive traits, and thus suppose

The dog-like ones – fine features in the main –
Not attributes to set our compass by
When setting out in that ape-centered quest
For human provenance. A canny nose

For scents and friends, a take on life profane
Though good-willed and forgiving, a well-nigh
Heroic sense of loyalty, a great zest
For life unbroken by the heaviest blows

Of fate, and a capacity to feign,
As well as feel, emotions that belie
The claim that canine nature's not progressed
Beyond the stage where food or sex bestows

A short-lived satisfaction. It will pain
Poor Emma, I suspect, but when I try
To think what moral boundaries I've transgressed
In my *Descent of Man* the feeling grows

That God-to-Dog's a journey through terrain
Where future glimpses of a common sky
At journey's end illumine what's expressed
Each time I know he knows I know he knows.

Truth, Love and Number: a colloquy

*The appropriateness of the language of mathematics for the formu-
lation of the laws of physics is a wonderful gift which we neither
understand nor deserve. We should be grateful for it and hope that
it will remain valid in future research.*

Eugene Wigner,
'The Unreasonable Effectiveness of Mathematics in the
Natural Sciences'

*Being true is different from being taken as true . . . . I understand
by 'laws of logic' not psychological laws of takings-to-be-true, but
laws of truth. The laws of truth . . . are boundary stones set in an
eternal foundation.*

Gottlob Frege,
The Foundations of Arithmetic

*The viewpoint of the formalist must lead to the conviction that if
other symbolic formulas should be substituted for the ones that now
represent the mathematical-logical laws, the absence of the sensa-
tion of delight, called 'consciousness of legitimacy', which might be
the result of such substitution would not in the least invalidate its
mathematical exactness.*

L.E.J. Brouwer,
Intuitionism and Formalism

*Numbers are not objects at all, because in giving the properties . . .
of numbers you merely characterize an abstract structure – and the
distinction lies in the fact that the 'elements' of the structure have no
properties other than those relating them to other 'elements' of the
same structure.*

Paul Benacerraf,
'What Numbers Could Not Be'

I A Dilemma (Wigner)

It works, but why it works we can't explain.
A mystery: ask any physicist.
We seek an answer, but we seek in vain.

How can we think it's real-world truths they gain
With all the math-based axioms they enlist?
It works, but why it works we can't explain.

Echt-Platonists, at home in ghost-domain,
Yet find the Forms reluctant to assist.
We seek an answer, but we seek in vain.

That's the real problem: doctrines too arcane,
Like that, can yield the physics-mill no grist.
It works, but why it works we can't explain.

Some say: keep maths empirical, abstain
From abstract talk; but there's a lot they've missed!
We seek an answer, but we seek in vain.

A flat dilemma, the logician's bane:
'Objective truth or knowledge', that's the gist.
It works, but why it works we can't explain.

No wonder puzzlers find the thing a strain,
Whether empiricist or rationalist:
We seek an answer, but we seek in vain.

Small hope we might yet reconcile the twain
Where each try warns the trier: please desist!
It works, but why it works we can't explain.

Cease hoping, and you'll go against the grain
Of all that whispers: try another twist!
We seek an answer, but we seek in vain.

For mathematics may afford the brain

A glimpse of truths that clash yet coexist.
It works, though why it works we can't explain;
We seek an answer, but we seek in vain.

II An Option (J.S. Mill)

Stay earthbound, make geometry your guide.
No lift from wings that beat in empty space;
No problem measurement can't take in stride.

Count, add, subtract, then multiply, divide:
The sums work out, they tell us what's the case.
Stay earthbound, make geometry your guide.

The physics pay-off proves they're bona-fide,
Though it comes down to simple stuff at base:
No problem measurement can't take in stride.

Those bother-heads need Plato to provide
A shadow-realm of Forms that they can chase.
Stay earthbound, make geometry your guide.

The rule holds good for maths pure and applied:
Look hard, you'll find a maths/world interface.
No problem measurement can't take in stride.

That's why you've physics breakthroughs alongside
The maths discoveries: it's a relay race!
Stay earthbound, make geometry your guide.

It's also why the mystery-mongers slide
From Plato's to the sceptic's tight embrace.
No problem measurement can't take in stride.

A simple point: if abstract qualms collide
With what we know then knowledge holds the ace.
Stay earthbound, make geometry your guide.

'Where things add up': please tell the swivel-eyed
Math-sceptics that's where knowledge has its place.
No problem measurement can't take in stride.

Why think our mortal reckonings serve to hide
Platonic forms of which we find no trace?
Stay earthbound, make geometry your guide.

It's here below that numbers must reside
With fractions, multiples, or lengths you pace.
No problem measurement can't take in stride;
Stay earthbound, make geometry your guide.

III Another Option (Frege)

No truths unless objective and ideal.
By formal proofs alone we know what's true.
Let sense withdraw, let thought display the real.

Why trust empiricists like Mill whose zeal
For Ockham's Razor sends their thoughts askew?
No truths unless objective and ideal.

Then those there are, like Brouwer, who say 'feel,
Intuit, live your proofs!' – a motley crew.
Let sense withdraw, let thought display the real.

I say: unless truth set its timeless seal
On all our thoughts we've not the faintest clue.
No truths unless objective and ideal.

Empiricists make sense their biggest deal,
'Facts of experience', but it just won't do:
Let sense withdraw, let thought display the real.

It's why they always reinvent the wheel,
Shun formal proofs, tout common-sense in lieu:
No truths unless objective and ideal.

Myself, I've long since silenced that appeal
To any sense-reports that might leak through:
Let sense withdraw, let thought display the real.

You tell me not to make a mystic meal
Of my Platonic doctrine: I'll tell you
'No truths unless objective and ideal'.

Those sceptics: all their sophistries reveal
Is just how deep in their own juice they stew.
Let sense withdraw, let thought display the real.

Grant them their faulty premises, and we'll
Be brought around to share that crazy view.
No truths unless objective and ideal.

That's why we Platonists need nerves of steel
To pay objective truth the homage due.
Let sense withdraw, let thought display the real.

For else those ersatz creeds would rush to heal
The truth-shaped rift in all we thought we knew.
No truths unless objective and ideal;
Let sense withdraw, let thought display the real.

IV Intuitionism (Brouwer)

Why opt for truth when proof's the best you'll get?
Drop truth-talk, Brouwer says, and feel your way.
No point just piling up an unpaid debt.

Objectivists have goals that can't be met;
They pitch the stakes sky-high but never pay.
Why opt for truth when proof's the best you'll get?

The trouble is, they place an outsize bet
With naught to lose whatever odds you lay.
No point just piling up an unpaid debt.

Our option leaves objectivists to fret:
'Go with it, see how thinking's led astray!
Truth may elude the subtlest proof you'll get'.

That's their big counter-thesis: once you let
Truth go the logic falls out as it may.
No end to piling up that unpaid debt.

So what? say intuitionists: no sweat!
Let your best hunch decide the state of play.
Why opt for truth when proof's the best you'll get?

Besides, how else allow for those as yet
Unproven theorems in our dossier?
No point just piling up an unpaid debt.

Those Fregeans think our methods pose a threat
To logic with its outright yea-or-nay:
They opt for truth when proof's the best you'll get.

But we think bivalence too coarse a net
To catch the nuances our proofs convey:
No end to piling up an unpaid debt.

Rather it's our intuitive mind-set
That has, here as in love, the final say.
Why opt for truth when proof's the most you'll get?
No point just piling up an unpaid debt.

V Love And/Of Truth

Where love comes into it's the question here.
Love-objects range across the widest scale.
Most holdings-true involve some holding-dear.

It's love of truth that makes the truths show clear,
Though sometimes (think of Frege) it may fail.
Where love comes into it's the question here.

Trust intuition and you'll likely veer
Too far off logic's course to glimpse the grail:
Most findings-true resist some holding-dear.

Take truth ideal and absolute to steer
By and you'll be a cautionary tale.
Where love comes into it's the question here.

For love long disciplined at truth's frontier
May find a dead-end to the logic-trail:
Most holdings-true involve some holding-dear.

Though Frege's case should tell us just how near
To full-scale paranoia this can sail,
Where love comes into it's the question here.

Still let's not treat his case as one of mere
Psychic disorder in the threatened male:
Most findings-true resist some holding-dear.

For there's no room in truth's exalted sphere
For feelings he decreed beyond the pale.
Where love comes into it's the question here;

Also the tricky question whether we're
Well placed to say where logic's wheels derail:
Most holdings-true involve some holding-dear.

One thing's for sure: no judgment more severe
Than his relentless quest that truth prevail.
Where love comes into it's the question here;
Most findings-true resist some holding-dear.

VI Plato's Shade

Make love your guide to truth, says Plato's shade.
'Perfection of the life or work', Yeats said,
Yet should love die, what truths shall make the grade?

It's numbers, sets, and measures all arrayed
In due proportion that should fill your head:
Make love your guide to truth, says Plato's shade.

Yet though that math-fixation surely played
A leading role, so too did love purebred:
If love should die what truths shall make the grade?

By shared participation it's conveyed,
That highest Form of Good to which we're led
By love as guide to truth, says Plato's shade.

Yet Frege's case suggests that we've mislaid
The key-word somewhere, lost the vital thread:
If love should die what truths shall make the grade?

That zeal for truth, in him, at last forbade
All thoughts by human-kindlier passions fed.
Make love your guide to truth, says Plato's shade.

The intuitionist replies: be swayed
By inklings, hunches, feeling-cues instead.
If love should die what truths shall make the grade?

Bring love's fine touch to mathematics' aid,
Spare no regret for old illusions shed.
'Yet what of truth, love's guide?', says Plato's shade.

'Let feeling judge and all the Forms must fade
To simulacra, like my painted bed,
Or images that no-wise make the grade.'

How keep them clear if love should serenade
Our thoughts until their content goes unread?
Make truth your guide to love, says Plato's shade,
Yet should love die what truths shall make the grade?

Ashina

My grandson Avery, aged around 15 months at the time, had a lengthy period during which by far his favorite occupation was to sit and gaze intently at the washing machine going through its cycles. He became quite distressed if his parents tried to distract him and was clearly much happier watching 'Ashina' (his word for the machine) than viewing 'Peppa Pig' or any other Children's TV offerings.

I call her my Ashina but that's not
The name they use for her, my Mum and Dad,
So maybe there's some other name she's got,

And anyway it makes me sort-of glad
If that name's wrong because it sort-of means
That nobody can share the fun we've had,

Me and Ashina. Mum told me it cleans
My shirts and shorts, my trousers, pants, and socks,
And dries them too, but I've seen big machines

Down at the laundromat with lots of clocks
And dials on them and know that's not the kind
Of job Ashina does, since she's a box-

With-screen like our TV. I've looked behind
To search for clues but nothing there apart
From all the wires and other stuff you find

On lots of plug-in things. But I can't start
To tell you what Ashina's shown to me,
This clanking dream-machine where head and heart

Find pleasures far beyond what kids' TV
Serves up for our delight. I'd say they sell
You short, those shows, because they make you see

Things their way, like it's TV's role to tell
You not just how it goes, the toddler-tale,
But where to laugh and clap your hands as well.

That's why I watch Ashina without fail,
Why, when they turn the TV on, I shift
Discreetly to the out-house and avail

Myself of her strange power to cast adrift
Those inner fantasies kept well off-stage
In TV's view of things. Then it's her gift,

Ashina's special gift, to turn the page
On shapely tales, set all things in a spin,
Bring wondrous noises off, and so assuage

My longing that tales end as they begin,
With a return to chaos where the dance
Of glimpsed familiars and the cyclic din

Combine to cause in me a perfect trance
Of rapt attention. Sometimes it's a scene
Where every detail falls into some chance

Configuration, something there on screen
That quickly, momentarily detains
My wandering gaze as it decides between

Those flickering gestalts. So thought regains
Ashina's magic realm, the freedom lost
When TV holds the fluid mind in chains

And all loose ends tie up, though at the cost
Of miracles that else might leap to view
From the revolving stream of fragments tossed

This way and that. Then images break through
Once more and tell me: 'We're the shapes of your
Fears, hopes, desires, imaginings, a clue

To every secret wish, an endless store
Of portents, dreamscapes, auguries, and signs
That leave you, cross-legged viewer, with no more

Than a vague memory of the tangled lines,
The foam-flecked whirligig, the ceaseless flow
Of many-colored stuff that redefines

Itself at every turn yet seems to know,
Like some pulsating Sybil, how you trace
An occult pattern in the to-and-fro

That holds you spellbound. Lost in mental space,
Drawn off on wild trajectories, you scan
Those depths of primal chaos for the place

Where your kaleidoscopic trips began,
Where first Ashina caught your inner eye,
And pure imagination first outran

Those story-lines you'll soon be living by'.

Five Topics from Adorno

1) Gold Assay

> *Like gold, genuineness, abstracted as the proportion of fine metal,*
> *becomes a fetish . . . . The ungenuineness of the genuine stems from*
> *its need to claim, in a society dominated by exchange, to be what it*
> *stands for but is never able to be. The apostles of genuineness, in the*
> *service of the power that now masters circulation, dignify the demise*
> *of the latter with the dance of the money veils.*

T.W. Adorno,
'Gold Assay', in *Minima Moralia,* trans. Jephcott

Deep thinkers talk of 'authenticity',
But we know that's the verbal rot
By which the fascist demagogues decree
We've no role in their master-plot.

It's just another piece of jargon, see,
One tailor-made to fill the slot
Where their kowtowing to the powers-that-be
Goes well with words like *Volk, Land, Gott.*

Take note of Rektor Heidegger when he
Reveals how language goes to pot,
With all those pompous jargon-words that we
Non-dupes are always quick to spot.

'In language lies our German destiny,
Our very ownmost sense of what
It truly means for genuine thought to free
Us from our thought-infected lot.'

Their message, bluntly: if your race i.d.
Or native language-ways are not
Echt-Deutsch then you can stuff that empty plea
And scram, you rootless polyglot!

Let's not deny: their language-pedigree
Is one directly aimed to swat
Aside all those whose tongue or family-tree,
On their view, counts for didley-squat.

So when they next head off on some wild spree
Of hunting out old meanings hot
From source, just say 'junk-etymology
Plus racist crap: your crowning shot!'.

They're all the same, those real 'authentic' guys,
They all think true-to-self's the way
To find the soul beneath the social lies,
As in some private gold-assay.

They're wrong because the self they recognise,
Or think they do, will never stay
Put long enough or auto-stabilise
To yield a solid underlay.

That's why the authenticity they prize,
That fake of fakes, must cause dismay
In any deep-self voyager who buys
Into its endless shadow-play.

We're social selves, existing in the eyes
Of others, those whose looks convey
Whatever fictive tales we must devise
To keep that wounding truth at bay.

Why not take it on board and recognise
How nothing now escapes the sway
Of capital, how it commodifies
Our lives, our loves, and everyday

Transactions to the point where 'worldly-wise'
Means 'giving head and heart no say,
Regarding men as so much merchandise,
And ordering all things just as they,

The boss-class, want'. So, should you think to rise
'Authentically' above the fray
Of inauthentic life, think how much ties
You to it like a tourniquet.

As Marx once said, no end to how it screws
The whole thing up, this latest mode
Of capitalist production where we lose
Our human traits, where goods upload

Them in distorted form, where what we choose
To buy defines us, and we're owed
Respect to the degree that we abuse
Our fellows as a social code.

'Be real authentic, self-invest your dues',
The gold-assayers said but showed,
To keen-eared jargon auditors, just whose
Crass slogans echoed down the road.

It's still the populist's most favored ruse,
That smack of genuineness bestowed
On trivial thoughts by summoning the muse
Of fake profundity to goad

The *Geist*-infected mob. Hear how they fuse
The lethal rhetoric that flowed
From Hitler's progeny with what ensues
When leopards ravage soul's abode.

For it's the same sound rings in their tattoos,
Those hierophants, as in an ode
Of Hölderlin when Heidegger construes
Each *Eigentlich* semantic node.

2) *Gaps*

> *Anyone who died old and in the consciousness of a seemingly blame-less success, would secretly be the model schoolboy who reels off all life's stages without gaps or omissions, an invisible satchel on his back. . . . Thought waits to be woken one day by the memory of what has been missed, and to be transformed into teaching.*

Adorno,
'Gaps', in *Minima Moralia*

One mark of a well-crafted text: the gaps.
'Leave no loose ends, let every link show plain':
A schoolboy rule, enforced lest they should lapse
From drilled routine to thought, the teacher's bane!

They're unmarked spaces on our mental maps,
Anomalies that tell us 'think again',
Or sudden jolts that caution us: perhaps
Our mental tracks are what derailed the train.

How often it's a trite conclusion caps
Some well-groomed passage eager to maintain
The rule: link up, avoid all booby-traps,
And keep those errant thoughts on a tight rein.

Totality's the monstrous beast that wraps
Its grubby paws around the teeming brain,
While thought disrupted fashions from the scraps
New linkages at each point in the chain.

Let paradox abound so thinking taps
Unknown resources, strikes a tangent plane,
Or stretches logic's tether till it snaps
And cuts across the rule-conformist grain.

Don't say: 'Adorno, give that stuff a rest,
Quit theorizing, life's too short to waste
On running life-experience past a test

That only you old egg-heads ever faced'.

Those textual gaps are everything repressed,
Struck out, distorted, edited, displaced,
Redacted, yet obliquely self-confessed
If with a well-trained eye minutely traced.

The true-confessors say: make a clean breast
Of everything, give auditors a taste
Of all you've been through, let us shrinks digest
The truth behind your psychic cut-and-paste!

Yet it's those shrinks, the 'get it off your chest-
Right-now' brigade, whose unrelenting haste
For closure shows how deeply they're distressed
By gaps of sense too large or oddly spaced.

For there's no life so uniformly blest,
Or cursed, that its five-act progression's graced
Like that of narcissists who manage best
With text and lifeline smoothly interlaced.

Strict conscience says: that one maths-lesson missed
Through sleeping-in is one you won't get back
In a whole life spent pondering its gist,
So set the clock and cut yourself no slack!

Too true, yet time may teach the rigorist
What gains may come of lives that veer and tack,
Or lessons lie in some forgotten twist
Of truant wandering from a single track.

Your schoolboy who goes dully down his list
Of tick-box tasks may yet turn out to lack
The gap-strewn work-around that yields a tryst
With truth down error's seeming cul-de-sac.

Blake's message: if the fool would but persist

In folly, then the error-toll might stack
Up high enough to vindicate the blissed-
Out sleeper, not the kid with books to pack.

Learn then from him the bad, recidivist
Schoolboy how those who take the teacher-flak
May earn, along with odd slaps on the wrist,
Some credit for their gap-diviner's knack.

3) Just Checking

*While thought has forgotten how to think itself, it has at the same
time become its own watchdog. Thinking no longer means anything
more than checking at each moment whether one can indeed think .
. . . As thought earlier internalized the duties exacted from without,
today it has assimilated to itself its assimilation into the surround-
ing apparatus, and is thus condemned even before the economic and
political verdicts on it come fully into force.*

Adorno,
'I.Q.', in *Minima Moralia*

You've caught me napping yet again – that's you,
Old teacher in the wily ways
Of dialectic, always out to slew
The course of fixed thought-habits, raise
The stakes by lightning coup and counter-coup,
Expose unguarded turns of phrase,
Show hidden premises not followed through,
Reveal the symptom that betrays
A psychic block, shift viewpoint bang on cue
To bring the dupes up short, and faze
Those predisposed, like me, to think they knew
Enough by now to self-appraise,
To make the grade as readers, fit though few,
Whom no such jump-cuts can amaze
Since having you as guide (plus high IQ)
Got them well past the entry phase.

That's how you put critique in first to bat,
By saying IQ's just a test
Of mind-routines or habits got off pat,
Of giving active thought a rest,
Avoiding any doubt-inducing spat
With dialectics, faring best
At thinking-tasks we've long been expert at,
Tasks set by those we've second-guessed
A hundred times, and showing it's old hat
To us, this endless need to manifest
Our role as thought's internal bureaucrat,
Poised at society's behest
To self-apply its prudent caveat
Against all thinking-ventures pressed
Beyond the caution: 'let him bell the cat
Who counts us mice with nine lives blest'.

Thought its own watchdog – that's the gist of your
Mind-wrenching text: to have us note,
And strive against, the thought-debasing chore
Of IQ tests and every rote-
Like mental exercise that tells us more
About what has us by the throat,
Out there and deep within, than what small store
Of wit it takes for some to gloat
'We're way up-scale', as if one's IQ score
Were what best sorted sheep from goat,
Thought's poor foot-soldiers from its elite corps,
And so ensure that those who float
Straight to the top are those who soon deplore
All risky ventures to promote
The thought that dialectic's mouse might roar
As monologic's antidote.

But then I think: that's one big reason why
I read Adorno, that desire
Of mine to test the speed and power of my

Thought-processes against his wire-
Drawn dialectics, or to come out high
On his thought-checklist, or acquire
Some trusty scale or progress-chart whereby
To match wits with the test-supplier
And so commit, however hard I try,
The same mistake that drew his ire,
The view that thinking's something you 'apply',
Some set of tools assembled prior
To any use you make of them, the lie
That has us ready reckoners aspire
To do no more than check or certify
We labouring brains are worth the hire.

And that's my point: so many ways they close
In tight to block thought's might-have-been,
Shades of the mental prison-house for those
Caught up in some crass thought-machine,
Like IQ testing, as the darkness grows,
Automatism works unseen,
And poor *res cogitans* no longer knows
What these forced protocols might mean.
Yet I think idly sometimes: 'Just suppose
Your quick-shift dialectics screen
From consciousness a protocol that goes
To reinforce its own routine,
A work-out discipline I shrewdly chose
To let me oscillate between
The restless energy of your thought-nettled prose
And my relief as test-scores intervene'.

4) *Splinter*

> *The splinter in your eye is the best magnifying-glass.*

Adorno,
in Minima Moralia

It's truth's distorted form they magnify.
No shard so small it leaves the optic clear.
A gift, those splinters lodged in the mind's eye.

Your views are error-prone but truth can't lie;
Sight-lines locate obstructions, far or near.
It's truth's distorted form they magnify.

Light bends at speed but these it can't get by,
Wave-blockers, mote or beam, that interfere.
A gift, those splinters lodged in the mind's eye.

Thought's optics tell us certain laws apply;
No room for pleading 'just my viewpoint' here!
It's truth's distorted form they magnify.

Trust lenses crazed or cracked to show us why
Things aren't and cannot be as they appear.
A gift, those splinters lodged in the mind's eye.

Take your first test-results and then retry
The test with splinter plus good optics gear:
It's truth's distorted form they magnify.

Those false beliefs you're eager to deny
Have their close analogue in vision's sphere:
A gift, those splinters lodged in the mind's eye.

For that's what best enables thought to vie,
Sight-primed, with ideology's false steer:
It's truth's distorted form they magnify.

Let thought find out where sight-lines went awry
And vision compensate where mind-tracks veer.
A gift, those splinters lodged in the mind's eye;
It's truth's distorted form they magnify.

5) On Truth and Happiness

True thoughts are those alone which do not understand themselves.

Love you will find only where you may show yourself weak without provoking strength.

Adorno,
'Monograms', in *Minima Moralia*

To happiness the same applies as to truth: one does not have it, but is in it. Indeed, happiness is nothing other than being encompassed, an after-image of the original shelter within the mother.

Adorno,
'Second Harvest', in *Minima Moralia*

It's truth that understanding falsifies
By holding fast to some great master-thought,
Denouncing error like a thief who flies
The scene yet turns state's evidence when caught.

Frame concepts as you may, they're under-size
And leak truth-content till the thinker's brought
To test what comes of thinking otherwise,
Of stretching dialectics live and taut.

The concept-master warns, 'Beware the spies,
There's harm afoot, stay watchful, clear the court!',
While dialectics ventures to advise
'Stay tuned, keep moving, jump the juggernaut!'.

For there's no understanding that applies,
No concept that fits content as it ought,
Where truth can figure only in the guise
Of what's squeezed out, distended, or cut short.

Who says 'I know the truth' is one who tries
To fob us off with untruths of the sort

That monologic fails to recognize
Since else its master-plan would self-abort.

Who says 'There is *a* truth', yet quickly shies
From stating it – from tipping its full quart
Into thought's puny pint-pot – snaps the ties
That hold us anchored fast in falsehood's port.

Give ear to Blake: eternity's sunrise
Is where they live whose aphorisms thwart
The Owl of Minerva who'd analyze
What keeps its dawn so dark and error-fraught.

So too with happiness, likewise a state
Of perfect truth-relatedness you bear
To life or love, yet cannot estimate
How much falls to your own or fortune's share.

Again, reflection always comes too late,
Strikes *après-coup*, bids consciousness beware
How its insensate meddling may negate
The happiness that once dawned briefly there.

Say, if you like, we thinkers meditate
How best to steer just wide of Descartes' snare,
Let cogito rest easy, and create
A space for thoughts beyond its spotlight glare.

Or say: the thinking-cap had better wait
Till happiness seeks out a place elsewhere,
A place where it can quietly contemplate,
Not fully grasp, how everything's set fair.

Check pleasure-quotients at the standard rate,
Not zones of happiness, since they're
Not intervals that simply aggregate
But moments out of time, beyond compare.

Bourgeois ideologues may speak of fate,
The lucky break, the moment rich and rare,
A fate benign in kind (though they placate
The bourgeois gods by adding woes to spare).

Twixt bliss and thoughts of bliss we alternate,
We prying housemaids, taking every care
Lest happiness exceed its use-by date
And thought give notice: 'nothing to declare'.

It's where thought meets a limit-point, where those
Thought-tantalizers, truth and happiness,
Demand it draws reflection to a close
And risks one let-down *denouement* the less.

It's how contentment happens, how it goes,
How stray thoughts find stray moments they can bless,
Not thoughts pursued with fixed intent to pose
The question: how conceive such pure largesse?

No 'state of mind' or 'mood' this thing bestows,
This happiness some gesture may express
Or fleeting tone of voice that no-one knows
Quite how, as knowing goes, to repossess.

The gap's an existential one and grows
The more as each new let-down brings distress,
Or each precipitous descent to prose
From lyric heights now offers no redress.

The notion of things falling out just so's
A large part of it, sanguine types profess,
Though casting back a warm romantic glow's
What underwrites its Hollywood success.

That frown of puzzlement is where it shows,
The meditator's quickening shift of stress
From pure beatitude, lest thinking slows
To zero-point, then starts to retrogress.

What they so fear is just what 'happy' owes
To 'happen'; how chance vistas iridesce,
Still points emerge amidst chaotic flows,
Or truths negated yield a hard-won yes.

Promises, Promises: a pantoum

*In the particular case of promising . . . it is appropriate that the
person uttering the promise should have a certain intention, viz.
here to keep his word: and perhaps of all concomitants this looks the
most suitable to be that which 'I promise' does describe or record.
Do we not actually, when such intention is absent, speak of a 'false'
promise?*

J.L. Austin,
How to Do Things With Words

*Austin does not ponder the consequences issuing from the fact that a
possibility – a possible risk – is always possible, and is in some sense
a necessary possibility. Nor whether – once such a necessary possibil-
ity of infelicity is recognized – infelicity still constitutes an accident.
What is a success when the possibility of infelicity continues to con-
stitute its structure?*

Jacques Derrida,
Limited Inc

Words live: mean what you say, say what you mean.
Lives change: the best intentions go askew.
No loss of speech-act force with shift of scene.
No telling what performatives may do.

Lives change: the best intentions go askew.
Words count: the darkest perjurer comes clean.
No telling what performatives may do.
No truth so weak it turns to might-have-been.

Words count: the darkest perjurer comes clean.
Past counting, payback dates long overdue.
No truth so weak it turns to might-have-been.
No end of saving pretexts, bang on cue.

Past counting, payback dates long overdue.
Word binds to act, whatever comes between.
No end of saving pretexts, bang on cue.
Let speech-acts hold and chance not intervene.

Word binds to act, whatever comes between.
Vows broken multiply, vows kept are few.
Let speech-acts hold, let chance not intervene!
Bonds loosen and anomalies accrue.

Vows broken multiply, vows kept are few.
Meanings perdure in contexts unforeseen.
Bonds loosen and anomalies accrue.
Good faith's the rule, not fallible routine.

Meanings perdure in contexts unforeseen.
Who knows when circumstance will stage its coup?
Good faith's the rule, not fallible routine.
The slightest jolt knocks meanings out-of-true.

See how the speech-act gremlin staged its coup!
No fixed intent controls the word-machine.
Your verse-form strove yet failed to carry through.
Words code for error like a faulty gene.

Dupes

The entire method consists in the order and arrangement of the things to which the mind's eye must turn so that we can discover some truth.

René Descartes,
Rules for the Direction of the Mind (1628)

Starting with Freud, the unconscious becomes a chain of signifiers that repeats and insists somewhere (on another stage or in a different scene, as he wrote), interfering in the cuts offered it by actual discourse and the cogitation it informs.

Jacques Lacan,
Ecrits

'I think, therefore I am', Descartes decreed.
Self-evident: no need to verify!
Voiced inwardly the words ring true and clear.
Who'll question this indubitable thought?

For scepticism here's the cure we need,
A proof that stands distinct to the mind's eye
And answers, safe within its Ego-sphere,
All questions cross-referred to reason's court.

Source apodictic, outcome guaranteed:
Mere logic shows the nostrum must apply,
That doubts, like bucks, must finally stop here,
With *cogito* our first and last resort.

Let sceptics quit the scene: no case to plead!
Just saying all's in doubt won't get them by.
Locked on to this, our one sure course to steer
Through seas unfathomed, we'll come safe to port.

Yet what if it's a text they all misread,
Those self-assured Cartesians who rely
On reason's claim to make the thing appear
A statement of the *a priori* sort?

So Lacan counsels: pay the text more heed,
Track errant signifiers as they fly
The signified, and treat such talk of sheer
Self-evidence as fit for Freudian sport.

Again: don't ask yourself 'Where might they lead,
Those trails of sense?', but 'whither now the "I"
Of Descartes' shifty narrative, that mere
Place-holder always primed to self-abort?'.

What if the *cogito* just serves to feed
Sir Ego some mendacious alibi
While, unawares, he crosses the frontier
To Id's night-class where riddling truths are taught?

Then we'd not think of signifiers keyed
To signifieds, or take as read the tie
Of meaning to intent, or the idea
That pint-pot signs each token one half-quart.

Let's then conclude, with Lacan, that indeed
Freud's lesson goes: 'just where I think that my
Self-grounding *cogito* has Ego's ear,
That's where Id's stratagems cut reason short

Since thanks to them, from such illusions freed,
Our vagrant alter ego may defy
The old Cartesian voice that tells us we're
Least duped when it's those stratagems we thwart'.

Rather the sense-glissade is something we'd
Best ride as Id directs and not deny
('*Les non-dupes errent*'), though Ego bids us fear
That life and love are what it brings to naught.

For, 'mean it' as we may, there's still the *vide*
De sens that twists all plain intent awry
Yet tells us straight: wherever *vouloir-dire*
Goes off the rails, that's where our words are caught

In vectors of desire that far exceed
The path-coordinates of those who'd try,
With Descartes, to arrest their wild career
By daylight clarity too dearly bought.

Schopenhauer: late thoughts (sestinas)

The method of viewing things which proceeds in accordance with the principle of sufficient reason is the rational method, and it alone is valid and of use in practical life and in science. The method which looks away from the content of this principle is the method of genius, which is only valid and of use in art.

In music we do not recognize the copy, the repetition, of any Idea of the inner nature of the world. Yet it is completely and profoundly understood in our innermost being as an entirely universal language, whose distinctness surpasses even that of the world of perception itself.

In aesthetic consciousness we enter that painless state, prized by Epicurus as the state of the gods; for a moment we are delivered from the miserable pressure of the will. We celebrate the Sabbath from the penal servitude of willing; the wheel of Ixion stands still.

Arthur Schopenhauer

I

Your man Charles Darwin has the right idea.
He knows that life's just dog-eat-dog at root.
A friend informed me, saw the book in proof.
Its gist: the species-race goes to the fit.
He grubs around, as English writers will,
Thinks metaphysics rot, and frets in case

The godly take offence. Familiar case:
Can't get his head around his own idea
And what it means, so bids us think that Will
Entails no more than having nature root
For its prime specimens. A doctrine fit,
I'd say, for those so metaphysics-proof

That all they want's the English style of 'proof'
Served up by endless hefty tomes of case-

By-case-type burrowing for facts to fit
Some given theme. No doubt a good idea,
Though far out-argued by my *Fourfold Root
Of Reason*, let alone my *World as Will*

And Representation. Proving – if you will –
Through metaphysics that all talk of 'proof'
In Darwin's sense is subject to the root
Delusion that defines the common case
Of rationalists and empiricists. 'Idea'
Is just the word both parties use to fit

Their lifeless concepts to a nature fit
For nothing but the motions of a will
Devoid of living force. I've no idea
As to what Will might be beyond the proof
That love or hate supply when it's a case
Of forces deep beneath that fourfold root

Where reason ends. Let my opponents root
Around for some life-episode that's fit
For psychiatric treatment. It's a case,
They say, of my attributing to 'Will'
Such elemental powers as lack all proof
Since purely figments of a crazed idea.

I say: at root all suffering's down to Will.
The symptoms fit: what need for further proof?
It's just the case, in no way my idea.

II

They speak of my misogyny, my lack
Of 'heart', my endless seeking-out of grounds
For discontent, and how I've raised a whole
Great creaky metaphysics on my need
For dismal thoughts. As if to say: your job,
As thinker, is to see the glass still full

Though emptied to the dregs, and not half-full,
Or (crush the thought!) half-empty. Yet it's lack
Or indigence that keeps us in a job,
Us thinkers, since it takes away all grounds
To postulate an end-point to the need
For fantasies of broken lives made whole.

I tolerate misfortune, on the whole
(No choice, you'll say), and much prefer a full-
On *Weltschmerz* to admitting some crass need
For comfort that would blind us to our lack
Of reasons to be cheerful. All that grounds
Such hopeful thoughts is the old Kantian job-

Lot of ideas – his best-of-a-bad-job
Attempt to keep Will quiet – on which the whole
'Enlightened' crew once banked as offering grounds
For reason, faith, and hope. Conceive it full,
That glass, though clearer sight would show the lack
That goads and sharpens every human need.

It's all in Shakespeare: 'reason not the need',
Cries Lear in torment, taking on the job
Of chief instructor in how far we lack
What's basic to us, we for whom 'the whole'
Can only signify a life-time full
Of defects, gaps, lacunae, missing grounds.

It's some such thought of nothingness that grounds
The Vedic texts I turned to in my need
For wiser mentors than those Kantians full
Of lofty sentiments (goes with the job,
Like 'Dr. Prof.') since seeing through the whole
Charade of thought's vain quest to heal the lack.

Clearing the ground's a necessary job
For thinkers when the need to 'see things whole'
Reveals in full the truth of all we lack.

III

I contradict myself, you say. I count
Music the highest of the arts since Will
Finds voice directly through the inner world
Of *Tonkunst*, while the rest – the visual arts
And poetry – partake in various ways
Of ideation and the veil of thought.

So, music reigns supreme; yet who'd have thought
I'd yield to that idea, rather than count
It more like hell on Earth, given all the ways
I'd gone around to demonstrate how Will
And its rough strife might cease awhile through art's
Too briefly conjuring a Will-less world.

They say: what place for music in that world
If music plunges us, beyond all thought,
Straight into Will's inchoate flux where arts
Like poetry or painting scarcely count
Since thought and image shelter us from Will
And so placate its pandaemonic ways?

Tempting to turn it round: 'among those ways',
I might reply, 'is how the ordered world
Of logic meets its nemesis in Will
And all the so-called 'laws' or rules of thought
Receive its body-blow: 'out for the count!',
Like old conventions in the sister-arts'.

But not for me, the logic-twisting arts
Of rhetoric and their beguiling ways!
Peruse my work, see just how low the count
Of faults or fallacies, then tell the world
It's clarity of mind and strength of thought,
Not weakness, that here meets the test of Will.

Let logic-choppers tax me as they will,
Along with self-styled spokesmen for 'the arts'
Who tend to bridle at the very thought
That music might disrupt their usual ways
Of thinking or of being-in-the-world
Till they've its curse and blessing both to count.

They'll frame my talk of Will in many ways,
The arts and science of a future world
Where id tells thought: no chickens left to count!

Quandaries: Fichte *versus* Kant

*The perfect unity of this kind of cognition, and the fact that it arises
solely out of pure concepts without any influence that would extend
or increase it from experience or even particular intuition, which
would lead to a determinate experience, make this unconditioned
completeness not only feasible but also necessary. Dwell in your own
house, and you will know how simple your possessions are.*

Immanuel Kant

*And just as my nature is posited, so there is also nature outside
mine, for my nature is not the whole of nature. Nature outside my-
self . . . is posited in order to explain my nature. Since my nature is
determined as a drive, a determining of self by self, nature outside
myself must also be determined in the same way, and this determi-
nation outside myself is the ground of the explanation of my nature.*

Johann Gottlieb Fichte

Fichte

What use your talk of ego's empty shell?
Your transcendental subject's just hot air.
How 'I' shapes self is ego's tale to tell.

Maybe it's sceptic doubts you seek to quell
By posting your 'X marks the spot' just there.
What use your talk of ego's empty shell?

Perhaps, as mere sensations race pell-mell,
It seems the one fixed frame that all can share.
How 'I' shapes self is ego's tale to tell.

My ego posits self and world as well,
Projects them both, a co-created pair,
So why your talk of ego's empty shell?

Untenanted, no place for 'I' to dwell,
Your living-quarters void, your cupboards bare:
How 'I' shapes self is ego's tale to tell.

Opposite poles attract, like poles repel.
So physics says, but physicists may err,
As does your talk of ego's empty shell.

Just let my Fichtean ego break the spell
Lest your net without fish bring new despair:
How 'I' shapes self is ego's tale to tell.

The rumour's out: in your great citadel
Of concepts selfhood's husks lie everywhere,
So drop your talk of ego's empty shell.

No wonder, then, if ego should rebel
And give you my *tu quoque* fair and square:
How 'I' shapes self is ego's tale to tell.

For it's the ego's primal glimpse of hell,
That Kantian answer to a hermit's prayer
Conveyed in talk of ego's empty shell.

Kant

I warn you: go along with this hard sell
And you'll have ego-trips enough to spare:
Of 'I' there's no self-authored tale to tell.

I sought to trace the boundary that fell
Twixt self and subject, one we thinkers dare
Not cross: best talk of ego's empty shell.

Parse *transcendental*: 'unit personnel'
Is reason's rule for games played solitaire,
Like morals. As for self, no tale to tell.

Should you seek an instructive parallel
Then lend an ear to Hamann and beware!
Why chafe at talk of ego's empty shell?
Of 'I' there's no self-authored tale to tell.

Thought-Communiqué: Nietzsche

In 1865, while still a student, Nietzsche visited Cologne, where he was taken by friends to a brothel . . . . In 1867 he was treated for a syphilitic infection which eventually led to the mental collapse of January 1889, effectively the end of Nietzsche's life, although he was to live, silent and lost in himself, until 1900.

John Banville,
'The Last Days of Nietzsche'

Whereof one cannot speak, thereof one must remain silent.

Ludwig Wittgenstein,
Tractatus Logico-Philosophicus

Some say such thoughts as mine must crack the brain.
My brain, it's said, pursued strange tracks of thought
Till madness struck. Another pet idea,
Much favoured lately, offers to explain
My silent state through some disease I caught
From that poor working girl, a souvenir
Of my first failed attempt to numb the pain
That came of nerves and intellect stretched taut
On paradox. All off-the-point, I fear,
Though why not give the fantasists free rein
Since there's no way yours falsely could resort
To claiming 'It's my life: the buck stops here,
You fiction-peddlers', flat against the grain
Of all my best-laid strategies to thwart
That old desire that truth shine bright and clear
Through falsehood, lie, and error.
                        'Too mundane
By half, too apt to sell his genius short,
That tale that puts it down to gonorrhoea.'
So say my future acolytes who strain
To outdo one another and cavort

With sense and logic at the far frontier
Of reason where truth's allies scarcely deign
To tread. That's why it leaves them so distraught,
My principled refusal to hold dear
Those so-called 'laws of thought' devised to chain
Free spirits down through logic's grievous tort
Against the wisdom, joyous yet severe,
That bids us redefine what counts as 'sane'
In Zarathustra's wake. From is to ought
Then seems a course that those alone can steer
Who've ventured out from reason's home terrain
After strange gods. Thought-voyaging, the sort
That changes lives and worlds, is apt to veer
So far from custom's sacrosanct domain
That, should its case be heard before some court
Of last appeal, there's no judge fit to hear
The differend between them.
        Ask again
Why this protracted failure to report
My mental goings-on – this many-year-
Long silence on my part – and I'd refrain
From taking sides in the spectator sport
Of 'Nietzsche: sick or mad?'. If they adhere
To one or other view it's in the vain
Attempt to pin me down, the crude resort
To bivalent truth/falsehood, or the sheer
Stupidity that clings to the old bane
Of Plato's heirs. This urges we transport
Ourselves beyond the dull sublunary sphere
Of sense and thus (the fable goes) attain
Pure soul-perfection. That's the lie I fought
By every means to hand, from those career-
Destroying early squibs that left a stain
On my c.v. to everything I taught
Concerning that long post-Platonic smear-
Campaign against the senses and the drain
Of strength, health and vitality it brought
To the near two-millennia fix that we're

Perhaps just getting over.
      Don't complain,
My friends, that I've elected to abort
That project: not storm off in some King Lear-
Like temper-tantrum, but thereafter feign
A cataleptic state as my retort
To those who lacked the acumen to hear
When Zarathustra spoke. If I maintain
A monkish rule of silence it's self-taught
Or learned from him, my teacher of austere
Yet orgiastic disciplines to train
Both mind and body in this strenuous sport
Of thinking guided always by an ear,
Like mine, acute enough to entertain
Such thoughts as lead the mental argonaut
Jenseits des Selbst. That's why I persevere
In my mute state, bear as my mark of Cain
This steady gaze that so disturbs my wrought-
Up guests, and speak in silence peer-to-peer
With those, like sage Spinoza, who remain
To vouchsafe truths no chatter can distort
Since known anew by each thought-pioneer.

Rules

I

No simple matter, following a rule.
You say 'rule n+2, no scope to stray,
Just follow teacher, as you did in school'.

Yet maybe someone wants to play the fool,
Or starts a new game, or declines to play.
No simple matter, following a rule.

Why lay it down that 'n+2' unspool

Exactly as the rule-enforcers say?
'Just follow teacher, as you did at school':

No doubt wise counsel, but the sort that you'll
Find otiose come rule-recension day.
No simple matter, following a rule.

Maybe there's some smart kid who thinks it cool
To take instruction in a different way;
Just 'follows teacher', as you did at school,

But sees it as his big chance to re-tool
The whole +2 numerical array.
No simple matter, following a rule.

Just look at those big-breakthrough guys like Boole;
Hardly the kind of precept they'd obey,
'Just follow teacher, as you did at school'.

They're more the types who'd turn your ridicule
Right round, leave you with demon doubts to slay:
No simple matter, following a rule.

All pedagogues can do is join the pool
Of communal math-wisdom, come what may:
Just follow teacher, as you did at school.

Not getting far beyond the vestibule
Of Hilbert's grand hotel's the price you pay.
No simple matter, following a rule;
Just follow teacher, as you did at school.

II

Some rules there are that ought to see us through.
Can't all change constantly as time goes by.
Things don't add up? It must be down to you.

How cope if five's the sum of two plus two?
Arithmetic's one place where rules apply!
Count on, and count on it the rails run true.

How think at all if thinking's apt to slew
Off momentarily on some blue-sky
Diversion so that logic goes askew?

Blame it on Wittgenstein; it's he who drew
The crazy inference: no reason why
All those rule-followers reason as they do.

Maybe a thing that loner never knew
Was just how far such sceptic doctrines try
The faith of trusting types like me and you,

Those who depend on promises or who,
If the signs point that way, opt to rely
On love's shared indices as they accrue.

Let's not pretend we'll never misconstrue
The signs, or have a motive to deny,
In light of some unlooked-for après-coup,

The pertinence of rules that self-renew
Or stay in force however far a cry
Time present seems from that set-fair debut.

Yet, equally, let's give the credit due
To players by the book who'd still fight shy
Of saying 'rules are there to break', or sue

For breach of trust if promises outgrew
The context of their making, or defy
The sceptic's rule of constant rule-review.

For as with maths, so here: there's cause to rue
That quick-shift way with rules that has them fly

The very thought of outcomes bang on cue

Or thrill to think that somewhere in the queue
Of numbers, out of sight to the mind's eye,
There lies in wait an unknown Waterloo.

The task of heading off that rendezvous
With destiny must be what keeps them spry,
Those rule-deniers keen to bid adieu

To any system where the fixed taboo
On innovation tends to cut-and-dry
Live thoughts into a robot retinue.

Still there's another side of it: take too
Relaxed a line on rules and you'll untie
Too many bonds and leave yourself with few

Real chances for the sorts of *jamais-vu*
Yet rule-based inference that no wise guy,
Like Wittgenstein's rule-bender, should eschew
Lest numbers, words and lives all go awry.

III

That rules change constantly some rule decrees,
Some meta-rule that changes with the rest.
Still let's not think we change them as we please.

Forget the maths case; he was out to tease,
That wise-guy kid, not out to pass the test,
Though rules change constantly, some rule decrees.

If Wittgenstein picked up that number-wheeze
And ran with it, let's not be too impressed,
Nor think to change the rules just as we please.

He merely deals in null hypotheses,
In claims devoid of consequence at best,
Though rules change constantly, some rule decrees.

For it's elsewhere, not in the realm of these
Conundrums, that the upset's manifest,
For us who can't change rules just as we please.

That they *could* change must leave us ill at ease,
Or anxious that this knowledge be suppressed,
That rules change constantly; some rule decrees

It must be so, though still the thought may seize
Us unawares at times, no longer blest
By that good thought: can't change rules as we please!

Rules are like locks to which we've lost the keys
Yet think they'll close or spring at our behest.
The rules change constantly, some rule decrees.

Partly they feed our hopes, partly appease
Our darkest fears; yet never on request
Since we can't change the rules just as we please.

Still it's the thought of rule-change tends to freeze
Our waking thoughts and leave us dream-distressed:
The rules change constantly, some rule decrees.

That thought's the one that brings us to our knees
In the small hours, by rule-change fears obsessed,
Since we can't change the rules just as we please.

But that's the thing: no depth of expertise
In rule-change method helps us hopers wrest
Control back; constant change, some rule decrees.

Best policy: I'll back the rule that she's
Now backing, one in which we joint-invest
Since we can't change the rules just as we please.

Won't have them say I can't see wood for trees;
It's woods of ours these termite doubts infest.
The rules change constantly, some rule decrees.

A handy rule: 'misfortunes come in threes',
They say, though 'count to three' seems risky lest
We think to change the rules just as we please.

Now thoughts of rule-change re-exert their squeeze
On hopes sprung lately in the human breast
Where rules change constantly, some rule decrees.

So here we are, all ready to reprise
The repertoire by which we second-guessed
This truth: no changing rules just as we please.

Rather they shift unnoticed, by degrees,
As rights and wrongs are over time redressed.
The rules change constantly, some rule decrees;
Still let's not think we change them as we please.

Last Reckoning: Hume

*For my part, when I enter most intimately into what I call myself,
I always stumble on some particular perception or other, of heat or
cold, light or shade, love or hatred, pain or pleasure. I never can
catch myself at any time without a perception, and never can ob-
serve any thing but the perception.*

David Hume,
A Treatise of Human Nature

*I have always considered David Hume as approaching as nearly the
idea of a perfectly wise and virtuous man as perhaps the nature of
human frailty will allow.*

Adam Smith,
'The Death of David Hume' (letter)

*I possess the same ardour as ever in study, and the same gaiety in
company. I consider, besides, that a man of sixty-five, by dying, cuts
off only a few years of infirmities. It is difficult to be more detached
from life than I am at present.*

Hume,
'My Own Life'

*I mentioned to Dr. Johnson, that David Hume's persisting in his
infidelity, when he was dying, shocked me much. Johnson: 'Why
should it shock you, Sir? . . . . Here was a man, who had been at
no pains to inquire into the truth of religion, and had continually
turned his mind the other way'.*

James Boswell,
Life of Samuel Johnson

No self, no soul, no mind-stuff to maintain.
Let go the thought of some Deep Further Fact.
For days they've waited, but they wait in vain.

'That's all', I tell them, 'just that endless chain
Of sense-impressions. Nothing to retract:
No self, no soul, no mind-stuff to maintain.'

The pious queue for deathbed-time and feign
Concern so as not to miss the final act.
For days they've waited, but they wait in vain.

They think that fear of death or mortal pain
Must give me pause, but here's my creed intact:
No self, no soul, no mind-stuff to maintain.

Of course it's their own souls they hope to gain
Should I lose heart and strike some dying pact.
For days they've waited, but they wait in vain.

If there's one thought now animates this brain
It's that no brain or thought comes spirit-backed:
No self, no soul, no mind-stuff to maintain.

They say: how find some order in the train
Of sense-events so fleeting and close-packed?
For days they've waited, but they wait in vain.

I say: let's cleave steadfastly to the plane
Of immanence where no such thoughts distract:
No self, no soul, no mind-stuff to maintain.

That transcendental talk was once the bane
Of scholiasts more subtle than exact.
For days they've waited, but they wait in vain.

That's why we atheists bear the mark of Cain,
And why they crave to hear my nerve has cracked.
No self, no soul, no mind-stuff to maintain.

Small wonder if I find it quite inane,
Their will that I affirm a faith they lacked.
For days they've waited, but they wait in vain.

It's odd, this need at death's door to restrain
My atheist jibes lest their frail nerves are racked.
No self, no soul, no mind-stuff to maintain.

Best keep the chat to matters more mundane,
Stay sociable, not have the show hijacked.
For days they've waited, but they wait in vain.

It's false friends and hand-wringers who now drain
Me more than how the lethal odds are stacked.
No self, no soul, no mind-stuff to maintain.

Perhaps they'll end by driving me insane,
That bunch, and turn to brute rage all my tact:
For days they've waited, but they wait in vain.

Yet why augment their whispering campaign
Or swell the gossip-sheet my foes ransacked?
No self, no soul, no mind-stuff to maintain.

Let's hope the pious brethren will refrain
From twisting every bulletin they've hacked.
For days they've waited, but they wait in vain;
No self, no soul, no mind-stuff to maintain.

A Plea for Invention

I

Ex nihilo creation: God's bad plan!
Things started to go wrong from chapter one.
It gave us Genesis, the Fall of Man,
And endless tales of providence undone.

Always the question where it all began,
What sent it off-course, slewed the opening run,
Decreed 'Think not the ways of God to scan!',
And ruled no upstart wit should jump the gun.

It's why God-bothered critics place a ban
On myths of mortal genius idly spun

By poets keen to garner what they can
Of godlike grandeur from Creation's sun,

As well as why the Faustus lesson ran
'Let your utmost imaginings yet shun
The fatal leap that binds you to the clan
Of Souls God-lost but Ah!, Mephisto-won'.

II

When Wordsworth says of Goethe that he lacks,
As poet, that unerring poet-sense
Of what belongs with what, it's his own tracks
He's covering lest the pious take offence.

For how else read a poetry that stacks
The pantheist odds, blends mortal time with tense-
Less brooding on eternity, and smacks
Of a creative will to recompense

Our finite lives with sentiments that wax
Prophetic, dream-projections more immense
For swerves of sense and logic apt to tax
The mind in quest of valid inference.

It's poets, gods, and egomaniacs,
Crazed logothetes, mad masters of suspense,
Who bid us flip creation's Filofax
And spurn the rule of cause and consequence.

III

The rhetoricians took a saner view;
Invention, not creation, earned the prize.
'Invent', from Latin, telescoped the two
Root meanings: 'find' or 'turn up', and 'devise'.

This rendered poetry the credit due
To ready wit while quick to recognise

118

How language services the poet through
Its gift of words for them to mobilise.

No thought here of the poet as one who,
By godlike creativity, supplies
A stock of visions each time dreamt anew
As ephebes one by one reach for the skies.

It's no sure route, the road to Xanadu,
But full of detours, swerves, and second tries,
Of chance ideas that strike out of the blue,
And sparks that flare as inspiration dies.

IV

Close reading shows us it's not metaphor
But that prosaic trope, metonymy,
Whose spinning-jennies line the factory-floor
And offer analysts their master-key

To matters some would rather not explore,
Like how the poet's metaphoric spree
Of world-creation cannot help but draw
On details chain-linked metonymically.

Imagination loves to rise and soar,
Like Yeats's dancer or great-rooted tree,
And not have its supply of bottom-drawer
Devices opened up to scrutiny.

For that's what rhetoricians have in store,
An undeceiving gaze that tells us we,
Though wish-projecting metaphors galore,
Must yield, with them, to crass contingency.

V

Not killjoy if the joys it would forefend,
Like some blood-boltered image out of Yeats,

Are apt to break the formal frame and lend
Their metaphoric clout to just those states,

Whether of mind or politics, which tend
To profit most from all that inculcates,
In art or life, a yearning to transcend
The everyday. It's how desire creates

That mythic-demiurgic will to mend
Truth's sundered sphere, or how it cultivates
The seeming power of metaphor to blend
Dissimilars, while metonymy frustrates

Its wish that allegory should have an end
As pure Imagination now dictates
New terms and Symbol bids us apprehend
What's veiled from all but truth's initiates.

VI

Invention, not creation: it's the same
Point Coleridge advances when he shows
Such zeal in disavowing any claim
To rival God by daring to suppose

The poet has some title to the name
'Creator', surely misapplied to those
Chance-gifted with the faculty to frame
Imaginary worlds whilst in the throes

Of opiate ecstasy, or those whose fame
Comes solely of whatever talent goes
Into the art, the craft or serious game
Of poetry. Still, you could say, he chose

A different line with 'Kubla Khan', less tame,
Less orthodox, much keener to disclose
The vatic sources and the bardic flame

That, with the breath of inspiration, glows

White hot.

VII

      His fear of blasphemy is why
The older, godly Coleridge shied away
From ever coming straight out with the high-
Romantic claim that had the poet play

The rebel's or the prophet's role, or vie
With God, like Shelley after him, to lay
Down some new moral code while governed by
No edicts but their own. If he fell prey

To a neurotic guilt that said 'deny
Your ownmost poet-calling' or 'betray
Your native muse', then seek the reason why
In what compelled the Mariner to pay

His debt of guilt off endlessly, to ply
The wedding-guest with his life-dossier,
And fix all comers with the anguished eye
Of sailor shipmate-cursed or bard *manqué*.

VIII

Theology apart, let's maybe dwell
A moment more on what's at issue here,
What holds that grey-beard in the endless hell
Of his compulsive tale, and what's to fear

From suchlike weavings of the poet's spell
Whose utterance, like Kubla's, bends the ear
In ways that leave us scarcely fit to tell
What demons haunt each side of dream's frontier.

The Peacock view may do its bit to quell
Those demons, the not overly severe
But searching satires of a writer well
Aware how odd his poets must appear

Yet feeling, too, how strongly they compel
The sympathy of readers taken near
The danger-point in their frail diving bell
And rocked by tremors in the psychic sphere

Beyond his comic touch.

IX

      This has its price,
Its hidden cost, the point that Wordsworth made
In saying poetry's no game of dice,
That Goethe's poems didn't make the grade

Since no prosodic skill or verse-device
Could make up the deficiency betrayed
By having shrewd interpreters look twice
For that 'inevitable' feel conveyed

By his own work. Beyond those caves of ice
In Xanadu, there's only time's parade
Of contiguities, the need to splice
Disjunct events, the dizzying sense-glissade

Of allegory, and poets' sacrifice
In letting go the symbol-wealth that they'd
Laid up in their not-quite fool's paradise
Where debts to time forever stay unpaid.

A Brief Collect of Idealism: ten limericks

Kant it was who kicked off by declaring
'Nothing real but in thought': very daring!
Yet he left it opaque
How us humans could make
A joint thought-world of things beyond sharing.

That's why they all had their *Kantkrisen*
When they read his *Critique of Pure Reason*
And discovered, to their
Intellectual despair,
That for sceptics it spelled open season.

The subjective idealist Fichte
Earned a place in *Ideengeschichte*
When he went transcendental,
Said all things were mental,
And so proved less *Denker* than *Dichter*.

The objective idealist Schelling
Found these arguments less than compelling,
Which was why he inclined
To give nature, not mind,
Pride of place in the tale he was telling.

Other versions kept coming: first Hegel,
Then Friedrich and A.W. Schlegel,
All testing their wits
On Kant's difficult bits,
Or the bits they saw fit to finagle.

Never fear: soon enough Bertrand Russell
Told the world 'all this Germanic fuss'll
Blow over once we
Get idealists to see
How it's logic that packs all the muscle'.

But no: Russell's heirs just updated
Those Kantian dilemmas, now stated
In terms analytic
But still parasitic
On all the old tosh he'd berated.

So, with language and logic now filling
Top place in each conference billing,
We're still up the same creek
That made Kant (First *Critique*)
The one father we'll never cease killing.

He marked up the score long before us,
We performers with parts in the chorus
Who must sing by the rules,
As in all the best schools,
Or have the Head Prefect deplore us.

Thus it was that old clever-clogs Kant
Gave his stuff such a bullet-proof slant
That, idealist or not,
Every shot finds a slot
That he's got ample headroom to grant.

Notes

Kantkrisen = 'Kant-crises'. A remarkable number of mainly German philosophers, poets and novelists had experiences close to a nervous breakdown when they encountered what they took to be the sceptical or nihilist implications of Kantian epistemology.

Ideengeschichte: 'history of ideas', 'intellectual history'

Denker = thinker; *Dichter* = poet

Lyric Suite: ellipses

I can tell you, dearest friend, that if it became known how much friendship, love and what a world of human and spiritual references I have smuggled into these three movements, the adherents of programme music – should there be any left – would go mad with joy.

The best music always results from ecstasies of logic.

Alban Berg

Alban invented an excuse to keep his poetic passion within those boundaries that he himself desired. He himself constructed obstacles and thereby created the romanticism which he required.

Helene Berg

I

My thought on bad days: Alban, you rotate
Women like tone-rows, cyphers fit to run
Through every permutation, whether scored
In love's or music's cryptic alphabet.

My thought on good days: Helene, all that's great
About him, man and artist, has been won
By formal rigors passion-bred though shored
Up hard against an errant passion's threat.

Yet still I bless the structures you create,
My husband, all those cryptograms you've spun
Round women's names, those women long adored,
Though safely, from a formal distance set

By tone-rows strong as marriage-vows or fate
That tell the clued-up listener: once begun
This thing has its own rules which yet afford
A counterpoint beyond our life-duet.

No telling Alban 'Let the row dictate
What happens next; let it ensure that none
Of those twelve tones recurs and gets to lord
It tonally. Else you'll convey regret

For music's bygone power to correlate
Tonkunst and *Rührung* so that everyone,
Each listener, might respond in full accord
As art and feeling paid their mutual debt'.

For thus spake Schoenberg, he who prophesied
Tonality's demise, decreed a line
Of true successors (Alban first of all),
And said his twelve-tone method guaranteed

That Austro-German music would hold pride
Of place for centuries to come. Incline
That way as Alban might, he'd never fall
For any such dodecaphonic creed

That banned tonality outright, denied
Its hold on our emotions, sought a sign
Of his elect vocation in the call
To cast aside all merely human need

For aural sustenance, and even tried
To stage a power-grab, one with certain *Mein-
Kampf* echoes, as a gambit to install
His progeny as music's master-breed.

That term, 'the Schoenberg School', is misapplied
In Alban's case when analysts confine
Their interest to the tone-rows and play ball
With his, the Master's, plan to leave un-keyed

(Hence tonally adrift on every tide)
Those future works where all the rows combine
In ways planned from the outset, hence in thrall
To acts of will no feelings can impede.

II

I said just now that Alban's passions ran
To zealously desiring all that placed
Strict limits on desire, or holding true
To musical procedures that require

(Just ask his best performers!) such a span
Of concentrated effort that we're braced
For obstacles and passions that break through
The lineaments of undeclared desire.

That's why they treated him, the Schoenberg clan,
As some effete backslider with a taste
For harmonies that might have sounded new
Decades back but whose date would soon expire

Once modernists who'd stayed out in the van,
Like Webern, showed how weak and Janus-faced
Was Alban's wish to stage a counter-coup
With Schoenberg loyalists in his line of fire.

Truth is, my husband was the kind of man
Who'd not see music's legacy debased
By factional in-fighting, and who'd do
What those hard-core atonalists aspire

To place beneath their peremptory ban,
That is, create a music that embraced
The twelve-tone method only to accrue
Some storm-defence as passion's seas ran higher.

They're noted down for all with ears to hear,
Those women's names, as in the *Lyric Suite*
Where he encrypts Hanna Fuchs-Robettin,
His latest sweetheart, with the usual show

Of overdone anxiety to steer
Us way off-track while analysts compete,
As he half-meant, to crack the code and win
Acclaim for putting listeners in the know.

Please understand: there's nothing I need fear
From so-called rivals, no way that he'd cheat
On me for real, just as the mortal sin
Of going tonal on the twelve-tone row –

The standard Schoenberg-Webern-Darmstadt smear –
Is something that lot endlessly repeat,
Thus neatly proving that the charge they'd pin
On him's just part of their recruitment show.

III

One thing I know because it rings out clear
In every bar: that talk of his 'retreat'
To tonal ways is merely how they spin,
For their own purposes, the debt they owe

To Alban as reluctant pioneer,
He who saw through the grandiose conceit
Of Schoenberg's fashioning. His works begin
And end in shared humanity, although

(Think *Wozzeck*, *Lulu*) no-one's gone so far
In fathoming the depths of human vice,
Depravity, perversion, wretchedness,
And all portrayed in music of a kind –

No, his uniquely – where from bar to bar
They streak the soundscape, like red wine through ice,
While tonal intimations seem to bless,
If fleetingly, the victims left behind.

You'll say I look too fondly on what are,
By any standard, sins that have a price
For me, his wife, requiring I repress
My hurt or anger and appear resigned

To serial infidelities (they jar,
These jokes, but let his wandering eye suffice
As my excuse). It pains me sometimes, yes,
As it would any wife, though now I find

Those names just part of Alban's repertoire,
Another life-and-music link to splice
Along with tone-rows, Bach chorales, and chess-
Like contrapuntal moves that he'd a mind

To use when needed. If young women star
In occult roles as sirens to entice
The Sherlock-analyst, then why distress
Myself on that account? I soon divined

How each appeared a new-born avatar
Of Alban's *Ewig-Weibliche* who'd spice
His fantasies and quickly acquiesce
In any game for helping him unwind

When complications turned out too bizarre
Even for him. That's when he'd load the dice
And give the world a fighting chance to guess,
From other names and note-rows intertwined,

Whose name alone subtends his *aide-memoire*
Of wished-for assignations, his device
Of over-coded clues that might express
A single truth elliptically enshrined.

Alterity: three villanelles

What is ultimately attested to is selfhood, at once in its difference
with respect to sameness and in its dialectical relation to otherness.

Paul Ricoeur,
Oneself as Another

Being alienated from myself, as painful as that may be, provides me
with that exquisite distance within which perverse pleasure begins,
as well as the possibility of my imagining and thinking.

Julia Kristeva,
Strangers to Ourselves

Opening the discourse of philosophy to an Other that is no longer
simply its Other is an accomplishment that marks not the end but
the structural limits of philosophy's autonomy and autarchy.

Rodolphe Gasché,
The Tain of the Mirror

I

What place in Ego's world for worlds apart?
Id knows the truth: its story goes that we're
Self-sundered, Id-divided from the start.

No Ego-healing for the fractured heart.
Alterity requires Id interfere.
What place in Ego's world for worlds apart?

No chance its daylight tactics might outsmart
Id's booby-trapping of the psycho-sphere,
Self-sundered, Id-divided from the start.

Id's votaries say blame it on Descartes
For telling Cogito 'the buck stops here'.

What place in Ego's world for worlds apart?

Let Id show Cogito the poet's art
As signifiers slide and rifts appear:
Self-sundered, Id-divided from the start.

One further jolt may send us off the chart,
Remove all compass-points by which to steer.
What place in Ego's world for worlds apart,
Self-sundered, Id-divided from the start?

II

Though Ego totters, still there's grounds for hope.
What harm should 'think' and 'am' not coincide?
It's Id that gives alterity its scope.

Where else but here, in Ego's envelope,
Should pockets of alterity reside?
Though Ego totters, still there's grounds for hope.

The alter ego, as self's isotope,
Keeps it with thoughts of otherness supplied.
It's Id that gives alterity its scope.

Maybe that's why Cartesians must grope
Step-wise across the other-self divide.
Though Ego totters, still there's grounds for hope.

Spurn Ego's call, 'give Id sufficient rope
And it will hang us both, Jekyll and Hyde';
It's Id that gives alterity its scope.

We're strangers to ourselves, and yet we cope,
We inner aliens, taking Id as guide.
Though Ego totters, still there's grounds for hope;
It's Id that gives alterity its scope.

III

No exit from the signifying chain.
Truth speaks in riddles: hence the talking cure.
Just listen out for Id's off-key refrain.

Hear Ego building up its dykes in vain
As errant senses yield to Id's allure:
No exit from the signifying chain.

They glance off its tight-cornered high chicane
Like comets on some wild galactic tour:
Just listen out for Id's off-key refrain.

Duped Ego thinks to ease the slippage-bane.
It says: 'may well-wrought senses long endure'.
No exit from the signifying chain.

More Id-attuned the non-dupes who abstain
From such self-doomed attempts to self-assure:
Just listen out for Id's off-key refrain.

Let its alterity spell out again
The truth that Ego labors to obscure:
No exit from the signifying chain.

Why humor Ego in that failed campaign
To keep the springs of selfhood clean and pure?
Just listen out for Id's off-key refrain.

No point your polishing the mirror's tain
If its lackluster backing foils the viewer.
No exit from the signifying chain.

Think not of loss; think rather what they gain
For whom this marks the Other's overture.
Just listen out for Id's off-key refrain;
No exit from the signifying chain.

Loco

Vandals have smashed up a model railway show, leaving exhibitors devastated and distraught. 'I trained as a teacher and a youth worker, but I'm in total confusion', Peter Davies told the BBC. 'Models that were made over years were trodden on and thrown around. It's total wanton destruction.' Davies said one club member had spent 25 years working on an exhibit that had been wrecked, adding: 'It's just horrendous. We will never have the time to build those sorts of layout again. That's where the anger comes from'.

The Guardian, May 19th 2019

There's something weird about it, something skewed,
You might think, or a bit 'new-male',
That unaccustomed show
Of shared emotion at the tale
(God knows it's sad enough) of how some brood
Of mindless vandals trashed the rail-
Way modellers' dream, a blow
(It seemed) to every 00-scale
Track-layer, signal-man, or driver who'd
Long wished to follow back the trail
To worlds dreamed long ago
And who now felt, in that wholesale
Destruction, how the real world may intrude
To say: your dearest plans will fail,
Your high hopes be brought low,
And your dream layouts prove as frail
As those the vandals stamped on, smashed, and strewed.

Yet there's a sense, in that male-only *cri-*
De-coeur, of things that touch some core
Of human need, that tell
Us plainly: these are toys we shore
Against oblivion, artifacts that we,
The makers or admirers, store

Away as means to quell
The fear that we'll have nothing more
To show for our brief lives than you might see
Consigned to any bottom-drawer
Of failed ideas. Let's spell
It out: those modellers implore
The tribute of all us who bend a knee
To skill, finesse, *esprit de corps*,
And willingness to dwell
Years-long on what they're searching for,
That last fine-detailed point that holds the key.

Who knows what other hopes or fears might play
A role in this, their endless quest
For a perfection freed
From time, change, error, and the rest
Of those real-world infirmities that they,
The world-artificers, found best
Acknowledged through their need
Not simply for some mindscape blessed
By childhood memory, but for the way
A favorite layout met the test
Of beauty, scale, and speed
Well-suited to the wish expressed
In all such time-bound projects to allay
Their constant worry: how time messed
With guild-rules long decreed
For those whose life-vocation stressed
A truth to details past, not present-day.

But, more than that, the locos and the track,
Plus all the scenery, the fine-
Drawn posters, track-side gear,
And other evidence combine
To bring it home that talk of looking-back
For some 'lost childhood' up the line
Won't serve to make it clear
Why others said 'Their grief is mine',

Why they too suffered that insane attack,
And how the value we assign
To certain bits of mere
'Neat metalwork' can still incline
People to think: such skills and man-hours stack
Up to a point where they enshrine,
Or seem to, what's as dear
As life to those now left to pine
For all that so enraged the vandal pack.

Sestina: A Shock to the System (Frege)

Logic and arithmetic seem to fit together naturally. Imagine then the colossal shock felt by Gottlob Frege, who had spent years attempting to prove that arithmetic could be based on logic, when he received a letter from Bertrand Russell demonstrating that his proof was fallacious. Something momentous had happened: Frege had collided with the limits of logic.

Alastair McFarlane

I'll not pretend it didn't hit me hard.
That Russell letter wrecked my dearest work.
Truth must prevail, of course, but it did set
My project back. Who'll say they wouldn't mind
If someone proved they'd given half their life
To prop a craze-cracked edifice of thought?

Truth's all that matters; clarity of thought
And concepts standing out distinct and hard.
So when they'd chide me 'Gottlob, get a life,
Get out a bit, get laid!', I'd get to work
On my *Begriffsschrift*, or apply my mind
To building numbers from the empty set.

That's where the problems started, as if set
To catch me out or agitate my thought
By some ingenious demon with a mind
To screw things up. Not merely make it hard
But fix it so the system wouldn't work
As those cursed paradoxes sapped its life.

Mine too, I have to say; the kind of life
Whose sense of purpose foundered on the 'set
Of all those sets (just feel its mischief work!)
That are not members of themselves'. That thought
Did so much to unravel all my hard-
Won progress that it near unhinged my mind.

The word soon got around, but I don't mind.
It's truth alone that matters, not my life-
Upsets or grievances, however hard.
If it's objective truth that you've once set
Your sights on, then you'll give no second thought
To who first got the thought-machine to work.

Yet that fine counsel doesn't always work.
Too often some infirmity of mind
Has me indulging the unworthy thought:
'Serves Russell right if nothing in his life
Quite fills the hole he knocked in his own set-
Theoretic project: hope he took it hard'.

I hoped my work might validate my life
As mind built logic's empire set-by-set.
Such was my thought, and its disproof comes hard.

Desolations of Philosophy

*Exploring the experience of dementia and loss of memory can bring
about a powerful, and vertiginously unsettling, way of thinking
about time, place and identity, where the notion of a stable reality
and a single self breaks apart. Frank Kermode called it 'decreation',
where words and meanings are unmade — an apocalypse of the self
. . . . This is a special way of being afraid: not just Philip Larkin's
furnace-fear of death, but fear of a profound loss of self.*

Nicci Gerrard,
The Guardian, July 19th, 2015

My life-world but with some quite basic bits
Gone missing, and this constant sense
That other parts, still there, have different fits
Or need recounting in a tense,
One missing from the grammar-books, where it's
A case of learning to dispense
With all those auto-reassembly kits
That bolster ego's self-defence
And shape anew the tale that best permits
That 'me' its dream of permanence.

My self's a bit like Mrs Gradgrind's pain:
It's in the offing, and it's mine,
Or seems to be, yet when I try again
To say just whose it is the line
Gets hard to draw, as something in my brain
Plays havoc with those byzantine
Synaptic links and so disrupts the chain
Of thoughts and memories that define
Whatever trace of selfhood might remain
To brainwaves grown so heterodyne.

Am I my own first person? – who's to say,
Since Descartes tried and failed, what ties
The pronoun 'I' to that fleeting array

Of sensory events that flies
Our conscious grasp then swiftly fades away
Before they've time to crystallize
In thought or image. Else the shadow-play
Might captivate our mental eyes
As Plato warns, we cine-gazers prey
To false ideas in sensuous guise.

Time was, time out of mind, when I stayed true
To my magnetic North, that dream
Of Plato's that had our best selves pursue
A path beyond the turbid stream
Of sense-impressions till we gained a view
That matched his transcendental theme,
An intellectual vista to outdo
The brightest visionary gleam
Of those content to see things 'with, not through
The eye' so senses reigned supreme.

'Retreat to Hume', the message went at first.
'Dump Plato, recognize that we're
Slaves of the senses, mindlessly immersed
In Lethe's stream where things appear
And disappear like dream-events dispersed
At daybreak. What's the use of "clear",
"Distinct", and all the thought-perfections nursed
By Plato, Descartes and their rear-
Guard cohort if it means we're doubly cursed
In seeking truths beyond the sphere

Of any sense-modality save one
That only mystics comprehend?'.
Yet now that Humean remedy's begun
To let me down and fails to lend
A show of normalcy to thoughts that run
On errant paths, ideas that end
In mental chaos, memories undone,
Blown circuits too far gone to mend,

And crass linguistic lapses apt to stun
Myself and skew what I intend.

For Hume can bring small comfort once you take
Away that communal accord,
That social bond that guarantees we make
Good sense to others, won't be floored
By such calamities, and share a stake
In every discourse aimed toward
Some mutual understanding. Should we break
That contract then we can't afford
To fall back, purely for appearance' sake,
On some idea of selfhood shored

Up handily by Hume's empiricist
Back-story of the means whereby
We gain from raw sense-data all that's grist
To ideation's mill. That's why
He offers such a helpful-seeming list
Of sticking-plasters that apply
To selves: through having those impressions twist
And braid just long enough to tie
Up in a tale with whose salvific gist
We're quick to self-identify.

'The Humean condition', someone wrote,
'Just is the human one', and their
Neat aphorism might have got my vote
As things were then, with lapses rare,
My syntax holding up, some handy quote
On tap, choice epithets to spare,
And thoughts that carried through, that kept afloat
From A to B without a care
For finding some Platonic antidote
Should soul's dark cupboard turn out bare.

But Hume won't do the trick once things have got
To this stage, once the social glue's

Long hardened or dissolved, the vacant slot
Lacks words to suit until you lose
The listener's ear, and finally you've not
Retained the least idea just whose
These words of yours might be, or what
They mean, or where to look for clues
To how it might unfold, this secret plot
That soon outwits your every ruse.

'Association', that's the single word
For both those Humean safety-nets,
That is, the sense of commonality conferred
By any social tie that lets
You feel assured you're truly seen and heard
For who you are, and then those sets
Of mental linkage meant to undergird
A fragile self that's owned its debts
To Hume's sense-bundle theory and averred
Its scaled-down role without regrets.

Plato to Hume's a journey that entailed
Some loss of pride, though it left room
At least for honoring the god that failed,
The un-souled self, by asking whom
Or what we might yet count on when assailed
By doubts. But now I read self's doom
In each word-choice not accurately nailed,
Each sentence rushed lest silence loom,
And every nascent train of thought derailed
By accidents unknown to Hume

With his advantages. I mean, his lack
Of psychic snags or kinks, his well-
Accustomed sense of how to keep on track
By switching the Platonic spell
Of soul-speak for the socializer's knack
For knowing what the mind can tell
Of its own workings if you just change tack,

Keep lively company, don't dwell
On private stuff, and get some good sense back
Inside the Descartes citadel.

So here I am, one who, as Lear laments,
'Has ever but slenderly known
Himself', yet now belatedly repents
His steering-clear of this dark zone
Where people, words, ideas, and past events
Leave little trace since lately flown
Beyond the shrinking space where mind presents
A recollection that's my own,
Or near enough to count for all intents
And purposes as mine alone.

Now nothing serves, none of those fine ideas
Spun by philosophers whose chief
Desire was to placate their own worst fears,
Or raise their hopes, or bring relief
As rumors filtered back from the frontiers
Of that dark, unexplored massif
Where every mental landmark disappears,
Which sends no spies we might debrief,
And whence we glimpse, as self's agenda clears,
What lay beyond its barrier reef.

The Ontology of Art: six submissions

1. Poet to Painter

'It must be abstract', as the poet said.
No painting, pot or sculpture makes the grade.
What use have we for Plato's painted bed?

Our poetry takes wing as soon as read,
Like Yeats's body-soul to music swayed:
'It must be abstract', as the poet said.

So many kinds of mishap they must dread
Who ply the painter's, not the poet's trade.
What use have we for Plato's painted bed?

Our art alone has wherewithal to shed
The sorts of stuff that crumble, crack, and fade.
'It must be abstract', as the poet said.

'No things but in ideas' we say, instead
Of 'things first', like the Imagist brigade.
What use have we for Plato's painted bed?

No eye so keen but bids we use our head
Lest we repeat the same mistake they made:
'It must be abstract', as the poet said.

Let's grant he saw it standing there, that red
Wheelbarrow; still no conjuring the shade.
What use have we for Plato's painted bed?

Though some may ask themselves 'whither is fled
The visionary gleam?', they're self-betrayed:
'It must be abstract', as the poet said.

It's that crude picture-theory must have led
Them to seek out the painter's accolade.
What use have we for Plato's painted bed?

Ut pictura poesis: if they're fed
That line it's thinking's role that's underplayed:
'It must be abstract', as the poet said.

Plain false that poetry goes best if wed
To picture-words that call a spade a spade.
What use have we for Plato's painted bed?
'It must be abstract', as the poet said.

2. Painter to Poet

Don't kid yourself: words perish soon enough.
Fine-tune them as you may, they'll not endure.
Each vowel-shift says it's all just language-stuff.

They give way when the going gets too rough,
When mere diachrony leaves sense unsure.
Don't kid yourself: words perish soon enough.

Each change of usage calls the poet's bluff;
Your tricks of form afford no lasting cure.
Each vowel-shift says it's all just language-stuff.

If the best rhymes turn up right off the cuff
Then classic-talk's a trifle premature.
Don't kid yourself: words perish soon enough.

Best take my words to heart, however tough
The gist: reject that old Platonic lure!
Each vowel-shift says it's all just language-stuff.

Let's get this right: not sheer linguistic fluff,
Your poems, but semantically impure.
Don't kid yourself: words perish soon enough.

Inverted Platonism's just a puff
For goods displayed in every verse-brochure.
Each vowel-shift says it's all just language-stuff.

Why take what I say as a rude rebuff
And cling to wishful thoughts you'd best abjure?
Don't kid yourself: words perish soon enough.

Else you may find the truth is apt to snuff
Out every bright star in your quadrature.
Each vowel-shift says it's all just language-stuff.
Don't kid yourself: words perish soon enough.

3. Composer to Poet

They got it right, the tribe of Mallarmé.
They saw that music was the Holy Grail.
Let sound and form shape content as they may.

Wagner's *Gesamtkunstwerk*'s the only way;
French Symbolism on a vaster scale.
They got it right, the tribe of Mallarmé.

Though poets have some splendid things to say
Their splendour fades along the language-trail.
Let sound and form shape content as they may.

Our works endure while words of yours are prey
To time and its semantic car-boot sale.
They got it right, the tribe of Mallarmé.

It's form alone that keeps the threat at bay,
Plus meanings too precise for words to nail;
Let sound and form shape content as they may.

This year's *trouvaille* becomes next year's cliché
As poets fashion words to no avail.
They got it right, the tribe of Mallarmé.

They got it right because all words decay
And so refute the poet's' fairy-tale.
'Let sound and form shape content as they may',

The Symbolist agenda went, but they
Were poets, stuck with words, so sure to fail.
Still they were right, the tribe of Mallarmé.

Maybe his flower, 'absente de tous bouquets',
Already bore a fragrance slightly stale.
Let sound and form shape content as they may.

That's why our notes have something to convey
Of what's beyond the poet's language-gaol.
They got it right, the tribe of Mallarmé;
Let sound and form shape content as they may.

4. Poet to Composer

Why think our art aspires to form alone,
That abstract music from a distant sphere?
Let thought, speech, music jointly set the tone.

Much better we should occupy a zone
This side of any mystical frontier.
Why think our art aspires to form alone?

If music's what requires that we disown
Form's debt to living speech, the lesson's clear:
Let thought, speech, music jointly set the tone.

Take formal purity as sole touchstone
Of truth, and chances are you've a tin ear.
Why think our art aspires to form alone?

Verse-forms may probe the limits of the known
So long as all co-drivers stay in gear:
Let thought, speech, music jointly set the tone.

Put spatial form in charge and you'll be prone,
Like Mallarmé, to have the linkage shear.
Why think our art aspires to form alone?

It's when the music-talk gets too high-flown
Or theory-hooked that poems disappear:
Let thought, speech, music jointly set the tone.

Tough luck for theorists once their cover's blown
And they've no compass-points by which to steer.
Why think our art aspires to form alone?

No help from that direction if you've thrown
All else away in quest of one Idea.
Let thought, speech, music jointly set the tone.

Best not convince yourself that you've outgrown
All that while boldly bringing up the rear:
Why think our art aspires to form alone?

Else it's odds-on you'll turn out one more clone
Of Mallarmé, to cap your verse-career.
Let thought, speech, music jointly set the tone;
Why think our art aspires to form alone?

5. Painter to Composer

Hear how the rags of time hang on each note.
To every melody they clutch and cling.
For future ravages, what antidote?

No use those endless labours you devote
To master-scores that notate everything:
Hear how the rags of time hang on each note.

Just play the piece again, and what you wrote
Sounds as if processed via the I Ching.
For future ravages, what antidote?

Though music won the Auden prize as (quote)
An art of 'pure contraption', here's the sting:
Hear how the rags of time hang on each note.

We drift down-river on a leaky boat,
Us two, and cannot know what time may bring.
For future ravages, what antidote?

So if it's on such shifting tides we float
Then risk attends your every tonal fling.
Hear how the rags of time hang on each note.

Still, it's no wish of mine to get your goat
By voicing truths with all too harsh a ring.
For future ravages, what antidote?

Just that our twin arts share the asymptote
Of things whose Fall's prefigured in their Spring:
Hear how the rags of time hang on each note.

Let's have no more of doctrines that promote
Keats' 'ditties of no tone' no voice can sing.
For future ravages, what antidote?

That's where you get it wrong: through your turncoat
Desire that sense-appeal play second string.
Hear how the rags of time hang on each note.

You think this adds a bit more puff to bloat
The culture-stock of all that music-bling:
For future ravages, what antidote?

But that's a thought you've likely got by rote
To elevate your latest offering.
See how the rags of time hang on each note;
For future ravages, what antidote?

6. Composer to Painter

No rivalry where no horizons meet.
It's hybrid forms conflict, not thoroughbred.
How judge where isolation's so complete?

The critics think there must be bounds to beat
But will keep mixing predicates instead.
No rivalry where no horizons meet.

See how their phrasing half-admits defeat:
An art of 'form in motion', Hanslick said.
How judge where isolation's so complete?

When you and I survey the balance-sheet
It's whole ontologies go head-to-head:
No rivalry where no horizons meet.

If those fool commentators think to treat
It as some petty feud, then they're misled:
How judge where isolation's so complete?

Granted, I'm not immune to the conceit
Of 'music first!', but just take that as read:
No rivalry where no horizons meet.

Say 'painting first!' and I'll turn up the heat,
Though really it's a habit I'd best shed:
How judge where isolation's so complete?

Read Lessing and he'll tell you how discrete
Are static arts from those with time-line spread.
No rivalry where no horizons meet.

Maybe we'd render warfare obsolete
If we could just put art-world tiffs to bed.
How judge where isolation's so complete?

Small hope of that: no truce so bittersweet
As that which comes when pseudo-feuds go dead.
No rivalry where no horizons meet.

Ontology's the safest place to greet
Those in whose service once you struck or bled:
How judge where isolation's so complete?

Still – see above – these *contretemps* are meat
And drink for those to their own art close-wed.
'No rivalry where no horizons meet'

Is none the less a slogan to repeat,
As here, when partisans start seeing red.
How judge where isolation's so complete?
No rivalry where no horizons meet.

Intervals

It stretched from 'Sumer is Icumen in'
To Frederick Delius's *First Cuckoo*;
That 'Little Winter' saw the frosts arrive
Much sooner, saw the rainfall waterlog
The fields, and Summer steadily contract
Till shift of season scotched the fragile seed.

Some say it shows how social shifts begin
When nature's hand obliges us to do
The more with less, like workers in a hive,
Or hearts with silted arteries to unclog,
Or birds that fly migration routes untracked
And vast beyond the habits of their breed.

It's where things modern have their origin,
So experts say, all those achievements due
To novel challenges we duly strive
To meet by planting grapevines in a bog,
By farming country where the odds are stacked
Against, and making 'don't give in' our creed.

Of course it's an old tale the masters spin,
The one that goes 'Behold, we've battled through

The worst of times, we humans who contrive
Solutions to all problems, and who hog
The limelight now because we've always cracked
The biggest ones with plaudits guaranteed'.

Peak cold in 1600, when the sin-
Obsessed American settlers learned to woo
Unyielding nature, find which crops might thrive
In climate-zones where failure seemed to dog
Their every step, and take on board the fact
That map-based indicators may mislead.

It's why, they say, the quick-change thinkers win
In times of crisis and – the precious few –
Come up with some procedure to derive
Good things from bad, or novel means to jog
Inventive minds and redesign the pact
Of harsh necessity and human need.

It seems the Stradivarius violin
May owe its unique tone to trees that grew
More slowly and more dense with no Sun-drive
To spur them on but heavy rains to sog
Their vibrant grain with overtones close-packed
In spruce and by pitch-perfect tuning freed.

That's maybe why they strike us as close kin,
The medieval round and that which drew
From Delius, four centuries on, the five
Spring-nurtured minutes of rapt dialogue
With gifts of nature humankind had lacked
Through culture-conquests seasonally decreed.

It's no surprise if history should twin
The big cold's advent with, as if on cue,
The growth of human efforts to deprive
Dame Nature of her power to bless the frog
And blight us humans, or her right to act
In ways that show it's a fool's case we plead.

No mystery, again, should pundits pin
The start-and-finish dates (marked hurrah-boo
Or boo-hurrah) at those times most alive
With fear and hope, when listeners agog
At climate-change found music an exact
Though cryptic guide that they alone could read.

Saving the Text (Kierkegaard): sestinas

*I held out Either/Or to the world in my left hand, and in my right
the Two Edifying Discourses; but all, or as good as all, grasped
with their right what I held in my left. I had made up my mind
before God what I should do: I staked my case on the Two Edifying
Discourses; but I understood perfectly that only very few under-
stood them.*

Kierkegaard,
The Point of View for My Work As an Author

*There is no precautionary measure – ever – that is capable of guar-
anteeing in an absolute sense the earnestness of a given discourse.*

Sylviane Agacinski,
Aparté: conceptions et morts de Sören Kierkegaard

No hope for those who cannot learn to read.
Salvation brooks no 'on the other hand'.
It's up to you: peruse *The Point of View
For My Work As an Author*, then decide
As you see fit. No get-out clauses left,
Just the one choice: shall faith now set you right?

Yet it's the works I proffered with my right
Hand that you crafty scanners choose to read
Ironically, or take up with your left,
And so ensure you've artful ploys in hand
For that unending failure to decide
When called upon that marks the aesthete's view.

Then you retort: 'but every shift of view
In texts like *Either/Or* shows we've the right,
As clued-up readers, sometimes to decide
Against your wishes. We may choose to read
In ways that don't come down to second-hand
Renditions of some study-guide you've left

To wean us deconstructors off our left-
Field strategies, our *n'y a pas d'hors-texte* view,
And do God's work by taking us in hand,
Straight talk at last'. I say: just get me right
On my own edifying terms, just read
Those boring works of mine, and then decide

As Knights of Faith apply the term 'decide',
Not you aesthetic types. You'll find I've left
The life-path stages marked up plain to read
For those who've come around to either view,
The strivers for redemption on my right,
The skivers chancing all on the left hand

Of exegetic darkness. Got to hand
It to them, those close-readers who decide
To call my textual bluff; that's me all right,
Read strictly *à la lettre*, but they're left
Up dead-end creek if we switch to the view-
Point of an author charged, like me, to read

God's purposes as those alone can read
Who pass beyond that stage. We know first-hand
What aesthetes come at merely with a view
To rigging things so they can pre-decide
Life's greatest question in the one way left
To ironists. They tell me: 'serves you right

If we stick up for every reader's right
To quit the passive ways you'd have us read,
To set aside those study-notes you left
And then, thus liberated, try our hand
At letting text and readership decide
What novel sense-horizons greet our view'.

But here's my question: how can 'point of view'
Denote a view from nowhere, one that's right
For nobody except as they decide,
Like my young man in *Either/Or*, to read
Their own life-choices as they might a hand
At cards or some quixotic fiction left

To its own plot-devices. That's a left-
Hand take on right-hand business, or a view,
Like Hegel's, aimed at giving *Geist* a hand
With some high-rise Philosophy of Right
While squatting in its shade content to read
Whatever trash the *Zeitgeist* might decide.

You'll say I let my pseudonyms decide
On many things, so there's a lot of left-
In trickery that gives you scope to read
The whole job-lot – not least *The Point of View*,
That trusty *vade mecum* – as a right
Royal licence for such textual sleights of hand.

That's why you say it's downright underhand,
My ruse for getting readers to decide
In my deictic place. So talk of right-
Hand direct discourse as opposed to left-
Hand subterfuge sounds like the God's-eye view
Of one who wills his readers not to read.

No tricks: I showed my hand; no ruses left.
They too decide who take the aesthete's view.
Their right, to choose damnation as they read.

Delayed Choice: Two Poems

1: Entanglement

The observer's delayed choice determines whether the photon has taken one path or two after it has presumably already done one or the other. The experimenter has changed something that in our normal understanding of time-flow has ALREADY HAPPENED. In other words he has changed what happened in the past.

Anthony Peake

It seems spin-values can't be in-the-source.
You split the singlet pair and off they fly.
Tests show they anti-correlate mid-course.

Some say it was no absolute divorce
Since measurement perpetuates the tie.
It seems spin-values can't be in-the-source.

At any rate most experts now endorse
Remote entanglement, and this is why:
Tests show they anti-correlate mid-course.

Delayed-choice findings go to reinforce
The point: no local realists need apply.
It seems spin-values can't be in-the-source.

Light-years apart yet still that quantum torse
Lends false assurance of a common sky.
Tests show they anti-correlate mid-course.

My question: what's this two-way Trojan horse
Between two particles that said goodbye?
It seems spin-values can't be in-the-source.

Perhaps it's not the physics but remorse
That says 'give hidden variables a try'.
Tests show they anti-correlate mid-course.
It seems spin-values can't be in-the-source.

2: A Quandary

> Your brain makes up its mind before you realize it, according to
> researchers. By looking at brain activity while making a decision,
> the researchers could predict what choice people would make before
> they themselves were even aware of having made a decision. The
> work calls into question the 'consciousness' of our decisions and may
> even challenge ideas about how 'free' we are to make a choice at a
> particular point in time.
>
> Nature, 11th April, 2008

They've done the scan and it's all down to brain.
They've done the scan
    and now it seems that mind
Kicks in too late to have a master-plan.

They said: decide on action of some kind.
They said: decide,
    then signal so we can
See if such folk-psy talk is justified.

Mind's prone to feign 'here's where the act began'.
Mind's prone to feign
    and consciousness to hide
Those test-results the voluntarists disdain.

It lags behind; the brain-scans can't have lied.
It lags behind
    and shows that we shall gain
Small comfort once the lag-times are assigned.

Their findings ran against the human grain.
Their findings ran:
        'all your fine thoughts combined
Won't help restore the high estate of man'.

Cast down your pride, with falsehoods deep entwined.
Cast down your pride
        and quit the dwindling clan
Of those who still take Descartes as their guide.

It showed up plain, spread like a peacock's fan.
It showed up plain
        and proved our mind-talk wide
Of any mark within its rainbow stain.

Just choosing blind or, at the best, one-eyed.
Just choosing blind
        is how we must re-train
For acting once volition's been sidelined.

Split-second span yet free-will's missed the train.
Split-second span
        yet mentalists must find
Some other way around the free-will ban.

Time was they vied, before this double-bind.
Time was they vied
        till cells fired sooner than
The time those button-pushers signified.

Thought strives in vain to stay out in the van.
Thought strives in vain
        when its last chance must ride
On bucking the communication-chain.

Let humankind not spurn what's cut-and-dried.
Let humankind
       give up that failed campaign
To keep its old prerogatives enshrined.

Too partisan we've been in mind *v.* brain.
Too partisan
       and stubbornly inclined
To have man out-perform orangutan.

Take it in stride as ghostly myths unwind.
Take it in stride;
       don't fear it's your *élan*
Vital washed out with mind's receding tide.

Haikus for New Times

Turbine

from seed to grass-blade
turbine blade from crystal grown
these twin perfections

Attuned

lark's song sheer delight
engine on tune pitch-perfect
such sweet harmonies

Cranes

crane stands leg-steadied
cranes rise clean above skylines
such fine equipoise

Spiders

thread cast across void
this webcast sent who knows where
reckless conjecture

Airplane/Seagull

trundler on runways
earth-waddling heaven-winger
saddest of put-downs

Bat/Stealth-Bomber

blind but for radar
day-stricken or dark-shrouded
sleep-haunting flitters

Tappet

clack of woodpecker
loose tappet striking valve-seat
uncouth intruders

Blackhawk

No quarter given
lethality their life-blood
death's skilled machinists

Aerogel

sky-blue aerogel
lattice of near-nothingness
cosmic dust sweeper

AI

silicon sphinxes
how answer Siri's question?
they will outwit us

Trojans

jet-trails write death-notes
sky spells out Cassandra's cry
we shall ignore it

Supercollider

each flash an impact
transuranic half-lives
nature's book not closed

Sybil/Alexa

jar-shrunk prophetess
soothsayer boxed and flashing
uncanny voices

Radio

Ariel's domain
'the isle is full of noises'
all's telepathy

micrographia

one chip holds archives
print books tiny as match-heads
world in grain of sand

Centaurs

cross-species coupling
heart-valves from horse to human
Ixion's offspring

More Topics from Adorno

1) Exile and Writing

> *For a man who no longer has a homeland, writing becomes a place to live. In it he inevitably produces, as his family once did, refuse and lumber. But now he lacks a store-room, and it is hard in any case to part from left-overs. So he pushes them along in front of him, in danger finally of filling his pages with them.*

> Adorno,
> 'Memento', in *Minima Moralia,* trans. Jephcott

No home but in my writing: such the fate
Of exiles, those like me whose works and days
Find habitation only as they dwell,
Though fleetingly, on the dense palimpsest
Of journals, essays, notes and endless screed
That forms their autograph and alibi.

It's order and disorder they create,
The comfort felt in some familiar phrase,
Some passage, trope, or thought that's served you well –
An easy chair – and alien thoughts that test
Whatever homing instinct you might plead
As reason to give some new place a try.

It soon piles up, the exiled writer's freight
Pushed on ahead of you, the stake you raise
To fix your mental motor-home and tell
How your cursed life produced an outcome blest
By writing's gift: survival henceforth freed
From the spell cast by history's evil eye.

Yet there's the catch, your thinking it's a state
Of mind, that gift, so bravely out-of-phase
With these bad times that it can lift the spell

By saying: 'think and write, that's how you'll best
Redeem your life of exile when they read
Those thoughts beyond time's power to falsify'.

For that's an ersatz refuge you create,
A lumber-room of scrap-books, dossiers,
Discarded drafts, and ancient files that swell
With ever more life-fragments, self-addressed
From postal zones where exiled scribblers lead
Dead lives as their dead letters multiply.

Let's not deny there's things that compensate,
Like the knife-edge intelligence that stays
On red alert for some faint warning-bell
Or any slightest sign that you, the guest
In a strange land, had better now proceed
With caution and not play the wiser guy.

You see the benefits in every trait
Of texts composed in exile: all the ways
Your style grows taut, your sentences compel
Close reading, and the labour you invest
In each load-bearing phrase betrays the need
To prize your secrets like a twice-turned spy.

No baggage-room on board, no excess weight
Or sentence left to stand if it conveys
No more than sundry mishaps that befell
The vagrant soul – of 'human interest',
No doubt, but mainly written up to feed
A vulgar taste good writers will deny.

There's something else those stories generate:
The sense that even life-in-exile pays
Its meagre dues to life outside the shell;
That anecdotes of exile, unsuppressed,
May let you feel for once that you've indeed
That much to share beneath a common sky.

Still I insist: let intellect dictate
What proper role such hopeful thinking plays
When you've no choice unless between the hell
Of exile and the hell that sent some West,
Like me, to think and write while it decreed
That others by the million stay and die.

2) *Truth, Beauty and Writing: two caveats*

> *The prudence that restrains us from venturing too far ahead
> in a sentence is usually only an agent of social control, and so
> of stupefaction.*
>
> *Scepticism is called for in face of the frequently raised objection that
> a text, a formulation, are 'too beautiful'. Respect for the matter ex-
> pressed, or even for suffering, can easily rationalize mere resentment
> against a writer unable to bear the traces, in the reified form of
> language, of the degradation inflicted on humanity . . . . The writer
> ought not to acknowledge any distinction between beautiful and
> adequate expression.*

Adorno,
'Memento', in *Minima Moralia*

Two points on which they're perfectly agreed,
Those bourgeois philistines: that no
Concern with beauty send
Their thoughts askew,
And that each sentence end
Before the complications go
Too far for those with little time to read.

Both vetoes say: much better not proceed
On that too risky path and show
You're seeking to transcend
What prose can do,
Or willing to suspend
The import till sub-clauses grow

Beyond the sharpest reader's uptake speed.

The gist: how such indulgences may lead
To brain-fatigue, as they best know
Who'll rally to defend
The reader who
Declares himself no friend
Of complex sentences that slow
Thought down or lyric flights from plain sense freed.

It's servile minds and servile lives they breed,
Those rules that tell us what we owe
To readers who depend
On getting through
Without the call to spend
Their precious time on texts that throw
Them way off track, frustration guaranteed.

I've told my Frankfurt colleagues: don't spoon-feed
Your readers, set the bar too low,
Or have them comprehend
No more than you
Expect should they attend
Just on-and-off and thus bestow
Fit honors on your undemanding screed.

Be clear: it's strength and probity you need
In writing, not the overflow
Of lyric feelings penned
In tried and true
Verse-fashion, nor the blend
Of formless thought with rococo
Prose flourishes to aid the case you plead.

Think back: recall that worst of times when we'd
A word-drunk, language-mangling foe
Whose every threat we'd fend
Off just by due

Care not to boost the trend
That made each excess word a blow
Struck first that intellect, then flesh should bleed.

Yet don't be fooled: the write-for-dummies creed
Is the same one that bids us stow
Our grievances, amend
Our terms and sue
For peace rather than bend
Our wills and syntax like a bow
Stretched taut to breaking-point in word and deed.

3) Snow

> In early childhood I saw the first snow-shovellers in thin shabby
> clothes. Asking about them, I was told they were men without work
> who were given this job so that they could earn their bread. Then
> they get what they deserve, having to shovel snow, I cried out in
> rage, bursting uncontrollably into tears.

Adorno,
'Monograms', in *Minima Moralia*

Still with me, that first sob of childish rage.
'No other jobs for them, just shovelling snow',
Folk said. 'That's how they earn their daily bread.'
The snow hard-packed, their clothes worn thin, they told
A tale of some far-off yet nearby place
Where justice meant such misery was their due.

No way those explanations could assuage
My screaming-fit, ensure I'd soon outgrow
The 'nervous disposition' that, they said,
Came from 'the mother's side'. So, five years old,
I first surmised: some things you cannot face
Unless with cries of grief – to them stay true!

This too I learned: that if by 'living wage'

They mean the debt of gratitude we owe
For jobs that leave us soul-and-body dead,
Like those snow-shovelers, then the lie we're sold
Is one that turns boss-class to master-race
By way of one adroitly managed coup.

But there's more to it, more to guess or gauge,
About my cry of protest: how a blow
To human dignity must conjure dread
In all sentient observers, how the cold
And damp combined to stress their wretched case,
And – truth to tell – how little we could do,

Us few 'enlightened' types, to turn the page
On suchlike miseries. An added woe,
Half-conscious at the time, was being led
To speak those words that seemingly enrolled
Me on the side of bigots who'd embrace
A code of 'just deserts', as if that crew

Of outcasts hadn't long since passed the stage
Where justice-talk applied. What I now know
For sure, I then knew dimly: that well-fed,
Well-educated kids, the sort who hold
Progressive views, may end up in a space
Where words twist sense and logic far askew.

It's half a lifetime's thinking they presage,
Those image-stricken words of mine that show
What demons loom when some unyielding thread
Of dialectic has me seem to scold
Or catechise lest I be caught off-base
By strikes and impulses I can't think through.

Sometimes I feel my thought's become a cage
Where passions pace, like tigers, to-and-fro,
Their eyes ablaze with anger pity-bred
For sufferings multiplied a million-fold

By capital's long drive to clear all trace
Of shared humanity from human view.

4) Schooling for Life

> In a real sense, I ought to be able to deduce Fascism from the memories of my childhood. As a conqueror dispatches envoys to the remotest provinces, Fascism had sent its advance guard there long before it marched in . . . . Now that [my school-fellows], officials and recruits, have stepped visibly out of my dream and dispossessed me of my past life and my language, I no longer need to dream of them. In Fascism the nightmare of childhood has come true.

Adorno,
'The Bad Comrade', in *Minima Moralia*

The horrors go far back, right back to school.
For years I dreamt of them, and now they're real
Once more; no Nazi commandant more cruel,
No psychic wound that time's so slow to heal.

Stage pogroms in your playground, that's the rule;
Start there, then make the adult victims squeal,
Or – failing that – inflict by ridicule
The sharpest torment flinching minds can feel.

I ran the action replay, spool by spool,
And told myself: no justice, no appeal
To some superior moral court where you'll
See them sent down to pay for your raw deal.

Fat chance: they're fish from the same savage pool,
The kids, the squads, the guys who made you kneel
To their vile taunts, and you the victim who'll
Forever feel the twist of that iron heel.

Those classmates often had the sorts of name
That rang old Norse or Wagner – Horst, Siegfried,

Friedolin, Jürgen, Eckhardt – so you came
To feel your victim status god-decreed.

Always the underdog, the one to blame,
Whether for want of valued skills like speed,
Agility or strength (just choose your game)
Or being good at those things they've agreed

Are signs of decadence or marks of shame,
Like speaking well about the books you've read,
Your love of music, or the way you frame
Long, complex sentences that far exceed

Their doltish grasp. Just ten years on, the same
Illiterate louts were those the Fuehrer freed
To drop such low-grade squabbles and now aim
At wholesale slaughter as their highest creed.

Some shrewder victim-types there were who tried
To get along by doing stuff to please
Teachers and parents, such as skills applied
To art or woodwork projects, though for these

Poor heirs of that old native German pride
In things well-made no stock of expertise
Could help to get their talents back onside
With boys who'd bash their brains out on a wheeze.

Another bunch would constantly deride
The teachers, interrupt each lesson, seize
Their chance to conjure chaos, then be spied
Carousing with those teachers, now at ease

With state authority since closely tied
To its brute exercise, to what decrees
Them its star students, henceforth qualified
To play Dionysius to their Damocles.

They step out daily now, from every raw-
Nerved childhood dream into the waking hell
Of life-in-exile, life that's all the more
Tormenting when you read the signs that tell

How home-grown US fascists know the score
And hang on, like my class-mates, till the spell
Of some mob-orator deprives all law
Save his and theirs of all power to compel

Where conscience fails. So nations stand in awe
Of fools whose reign of terror rose and fell
With each boy's passage through the class-room door
Or homeward journey signaled by the bell

That told us, falsely, how we might yet draw
Sufficient comfort from that prison-cell,
The bourgeois family, or just ignore
Those threats so long as our home life went well.

For if I've learned one lesson, taken in
From school-days down, it's not to fancy there's
Some world elsewhere, a realm of kith and kin,
Of restful sleep, a private realm one shares

With others likewise sheltered from life's twin
Afflictions, those 'political affairs'
That keep intruding and the 'world within'
That treats its dreamers to the worst nightmares

Of history relived. They'd best begin
By figuring out what happened unawares
And early on for us whose only sin
Was then to come of age when thinking bears

Such paralyzing strains, when any win
For prudence is a triumph that prepares
For moral infamy, and when the spin
On its dark tale is such that hope despairs.

5) Negatives

He who wishes to know the truth about life in its immediacy must scrutinize its estranged form, the objective powers that determine individual existence even in its most hidden recesses.

Adorno,
'Dedication', in *Minima Moralia*

He who is not malign does not live serenely but with a peculiarly chaste hardness and intolerance. Lacking appropriate objects, his love can scarcely express itself except by hatred for the inappropriate, in which admittedly he comes to resemble what he hates. The bourgeois, however, is tolerant. His love of people as they are stems from his hatred of what they might be.

Adorno,
'Final Serenity', in *Minima Moralia*

Why think – you good-news bearers – why on earth
Think everything's predestined to transpire
As reason has it, plus your tuppence-worth
Of bright-side twittering bred of heart's desire,
When all the signs instruct us there's a dearth
Of negatives, a stink of minds for hire,
About your always heralding the birth
Of brave new worlds although the times are dire.

O progeny of Hegel, think before
You hitch your cause to that delusive star,
That dialectic primed to fix the score,
Ensure that positives prevail and bar
All thought of negatives, of what's in store
Unless we face the worst and force ajar
The rusty-hinged, the barely outlined door
To what-might-be, shut tight by how-things-are.

It's hopes misplaced that send our lives awry,
False optimism put about by those
With most to gain that has us magnify

The signs of progress, thinking they disclose
The kind of future bliss long peddled by
The culture-industry to all who chose,
Or swallowed outright, its pie-in-the-sky
Fake substitute that led them by the nose.

Try telling them 'It kills your every chance
Of genuine happiness, that mindless pap',
And they'll have answers worked out in advance
By corporate taste-purveyors keen to slap
Down any challenge to their high finance,
Their hefty stake in any means to sap
Our mental powers by having cheap romance
And wish-projection stuff the thinking-gap.

'Relentless negativity': they bring
The same old charge against me, but it flies
Back like a boomerang since everything
They say confirms my negative surmise,
My case that it's those sanguine types who cling
Most tightly to their positives who'll rise
To any bait the culture-mongers fling
Before them as the losers' booby-prize.

For only if we think against the lure
Of those false tidings can we hope to gain
Some leverage, some fulcrum-point secure
Enough to take the torsion-bearing strain,
Unleash the negative, and so ensure
Truths glimpsed aslant, perceived against the grain,
Not offered falsely as a total cure
For false totality, the thinker's bane.

No prizes for those constantly impelled,
Like me, to seek out flaws, to tap the wheels
Of thought's great locomotive, find what held
The thing on track though every test reveals
Another crack, another system felled
By bad fits, poor materials, sloppy seals,

Or some years-long unnoticed faulty weld
Ignored as thought pursued its high ideals.

Some special positives there are that get
Beneath my guard, disarm the critic, take
Me decades back – like favourite poems set
By Brahms, each one a Proustian keepsake
Of childhood scenes and memories that let
Me, bourgeois as I am, enjoy the ache
Of guilty longing for a past as yet
Untouched by culture's all-corrupting stake.

But then I think: how keep it up, that last-
Ditch alibi of every bourgeois soul,
That spirit-sanctum barricaded fast,
Like bourgeois households, lest its social role
As private-property enforcer cast
An undeceiving spotlight on the whole
Domestic scene that Kierkegaard once passed
Off, comically, as spirit's aureole.

Yet there's a point where dialectic hits
The limit of negation's power to strip
Soul's vestiges away, where thinking quits
That endlessly renewed attempt to clip
Hope's flimsy wings, and where the force of its
Unstinting pessimism may just tip
The scales so thought's long sojourn in the pits
Can find new strength to give despair the slip.

You'll say: 'it's just a cop-out, that retreat
From your fixed rule so zealously pursued,
And thereby bound to end in self-defeat,
To the idea that thinking should conclude
Its *via negativa* on Hope Street,
Persuaded by a momentary mood
Of chance nostalgic uplift to unseat
Negation for some fake beatitude'.

I say: without that *promesse de bonheur*,
That fleeting glimpse of what life yet might be
In what our own life-memories confer,
We'd have no means at hand for thought to free
Itself from hope's unresting saboteur,
The negative that stifles every plea
For thinking-space by dint of *force majeure*
And locks it down with hindsight's master-key.

No contradiction here despite what they,
My critics, deem a case of double-think,
With 'negative' used mostly to convey
How thought dismantles falsehoods, link by link,
But then – just now! – with reference to the way
That capital and culture join to sink,
By serially negating, every stray
Redemptive impulse as life-prospects shrink.

It's bad faith pure and simple on their part,
That motivated failure to conceive
How taking thought may lead to taking heart,
How untruth's negative inversions leave
A lasting mark, and how life-changes start
With some snagged thread in error's subtle weave
Which, as it yields to nay's yet subtler art,
Shows truths no good-news bearer could retrieve.

Reading Together

Now, as he [Ambrose] read, his eyes glanced over the pages and his heart searched out the sense, but his voice and tongue were silent. Often when we came to his room . . . we would see him thus reading to himself. After we had sat for a long time in silence – for who would dare interrupt one so intent? – we would then depart, realizing that he was unwilling to be distracted.

St. Augustine,
Confessions 6:3

Strange intimacy, reading side by side.
'So close', you say, 'such mutual solitude.'
Two fictive worlds, no burrowing between.
Yet here we sit, each reading, each aware

The other must be dreaming open-eyed
Within their world, built strictly to exclude
All reference to the merely might-have-been,
The world we side-by-siders dream and share.

If I say 'share' then still I shan't have lied.
In truth it's more than just a tranquil mood,
A pious hope, or wished-for change of scene:
It's how things are when we're both reading there.

Dream-worlds and fictive worlds may sub-divide
Till short-hop flyers merely self-delude,
Yet here we are, two hoppers who convene
Across that cosmic space from chair to chair.

Maybe it's you, my trans-galactic guide
To worlds revealed as one when rightly viewed;
Or maybe it's what reading-sharers mean
By dreaming worlds together, pair by pair.

No doubting it, the worlds are multiplied

Beyond all hope of cross-points promptly cued,
Though still we break the law of quarantine
That bids us trans-world voyagers take care.

Let gods and old-style novelists bestride
The gaps where no-go notices intrude;
Let film-directors use their silver screen
To show those zones of privacy laid bare.

Meanwhile our reading-times keep us supplied
With cross-world rumours, momently renewed,
That leave behind the humdrum talk-routine
Of those with prime-time sofa chat to spare.

That's maybe why you sometimes seek to hide
Just what you're reading, so we shan't collude,
Like soul-mate stars in *Hello* magazine,
And shun all thought of reading solitaire.

For it's a vital thought that's then denied,
The thought of reading-time in which to brood,
Reflect, or let the fiction intervene
In ways your own, not all the world's affair.

Let's have those hours of silence still abide
Our question, like the evening interlude
Of monkish study-time that Augustine
Missed out on: silence shared, a call to prayer.

He witnessed Ambrose and saw fit to chide
The silent reader, though it takes no shrewd
Interpreter to figure out how keen
He is to skip that private-language snare.

It's speaking silences where truths reside,
Those inter-zones where reading can't be skewed
By any version of the lie-machine
That has us think: shared privacies, beware!

Roles

Just think: I've played a role my whole life through.
They've changed, but not my need for roles to play.
Adopted one by one, each served my need.
I fashioned them anew from day to day
As shifting mood or circumstance decreed.
No falsehood where no selfhood to betray.
My plea: *'Count me the sort of person who . . . '.*

The roles proliferate, the masks accrue;
How choose from such a limitless array?
'O friends, there is no friend': the case I plead
Tears pages from the old-friends dossier
Though role-change can, if opportune, succeed
In keeping friendship's treacheries at bay.
Just think: I've played a role my whole life through.

Fly high and fast: you'll get an overview
Of my big roles, reprise them as you may,
Though he who runs is likeliest to read
Amiss and spoil the living cabaret
With cut-out 'characters'. My friend, you're freed
To switch roles momentarily and say,
Like me: *'Count me the sort of person who . . . '.*

You ask: 'what when your life-account falls due,
When roles run out, when there's a price to pay?'.
There's how it ends to reckon with, agreed,
But also how, for shifters, there's no way
To dodge the choice, hold fast to last week's creed,
And have fixed dance-steps block your next sashay.
Just think: I've played a role my whole life through.

No fixed-step 'Strictly' code for me and you,
Us quick-change types who make it up while they,
The dancing puppet-masters, take a lead
In some minutely choreographed ballet
Whose every step insists we not concede
That role-play's everything, so no roles stay
The same: *'Count me the sort of person who . . . '.*

I switch them constantly: the me you knew,
Or thought you knew, now deems that role *passé*
And tries another, one more up to speed
Or better placed to cap my *résumé*
Of selves, or alibis, put up to feed
My appetite for gestures that convey
This much: *I've played a role my whole life through.*

It comes of asking always 'Will this do?'.
It comes of having past-role ghosts to lay.
The ghosts say 'Your old errors, pay them heed!'.
The questions hover round like birds of prey.
Yet it's fake satisfaction guaranteed
When role-personae fall beneath the sway
Of self: *'Count me the sort of person who . . . '.*

The oldest lie: 'To thine own self be true'.
No home address, all selves tagged aka,
'Existence before essence', first the deed
And thence the doer; heady stuff but, hey,
It's Nietzsche's view (and Sartre's too) so we'd
Best shape a role round each new sobriquet.
My truth: *count me the sort of person who*
Concludes he's played a role his whole life through.

Walking the Talk

The larval sea squirt knew when it was hungry and how to move about, and it could tell up from down. But, when it fused on to a rock to start its new vegetative existence, it consumed its redundant eye, brain and spinal cord. Certain species of jellyfish, conversely, start out as brainless polyps on rocks, only developing complicated nerves that might be considered semi-brains as they become swimmers.

Amy Fleming,
citing Shane O'Mara, 'It's a Superpower: how
walking makes us healthier, happier and brainier',
The Guardian, July 28th, 2019

I walk, therefore I am; I walk and think.
It's ambulation spurs the mind to thought.
Descartes got half-way there, but missed the link;
'I think, therefore I am': the proof falls short,
Seems strong enough, but fails to show they sync,
The 'I' that's object of that self-report
And subject 'I' who switches, in a blink,
To play judge-advocate in reason's court,
Assert 'I am', and hide the tell-tale chink
In psyche's armour. Message: don't resort
To mind as your last refuge on the brink
Of all-out scepticism if it's bought
At body's cost. For mind itself will shrink
As active locomotion drops to naught,
As cogito retreats, as neurons wink
And die, as software programmes self-abort,
And one last system-wide, mind-blowing kink
Delivers body's ultimate retort.

The humble sea-squirt's born with tiny brain
And, though invertebrate, with spinal cord
Plus basic nervous system. These remain
No longer than its urge to roam abroad,
Swim round a bit, and by those actions gain

Some new expansion-slot for its onboard
Computer. Yet the neurons grow in vain
Since, soon enough, the creature drifts toward
Some handy rock, makes that its home domain,
Clings limpet-like and then, if tides afford
No passing plankton, bucks the seafood-chain
By dumping any IQ-points it scored,
Re-running Darwin's tale against the grain,
And making brain and spine a smorgasbord
For its own sustenance. The lesson's plain
For you Cartesians: what you've ignored,
Perversely, is the desk-bound thinker's bane,
The sovereign intellect as two-edged sword.

Your jellyfish presents a striking case
To contrary effect since it's no more,
To start with, than a see-through waste of space,
A brainless, sightless, nerveless metaphor
For every undead thing that bears no trace
Of innervation, or the buzzing store
Of species-knowledge that accrues apace
In living creatures. Yet, till washed ashore
To die, it somehow swims from place to place,
Seeks out new shoals and sea-beds to explore,
And so acquires in a short time, by grace
Of such activity, that which before
It neither had nor needed. Go off-base,
Some instinct says, get bearings, pop next-door
And find, if briefly, how the interface
Of world and creature brings a new *rapport*
As neurons learn, through movement, to embrace
A sense of unknown possibles in store.

We walk together talking, you and I,
Our steps and talk in unforced synchrony
As landmarks, scenes and episodes pass by
At their own pace. Already we foresee
A time to come when memories multiply

And intertwine so we've some headroom free
For what remains to us of of earth, sea, sky
Or recollected words that hold the key
To mindscapes further back. Same points apply
To us as to the whole menagerie,
The big land-lubbers and the smaller fry
Right down to those rock-polyps. Think how we
Co-ambulated till (it seems to my
Re-wakened sense of things) the you-and-me
Of lives apart was soon left high and dry,
Like a beached jellyfish, while we'd a sea
Of creaturely potential yet to try
As neurons mapped excursions yet to be.

Consequences

For Dennis Fairfield, 1932-2019

If I'd not phoned then you'd be living still.
You woke, rose, stumbled, fell, and there you lay.
How reckon consequences, good or ill?

I run the usual self-exempting drill:
'No blame for unforseeables, no way'.
If I'd not phoned then you'd be living still.

I say 'but killing is an act of will,
Not tied to lethal upshots come what may;
How reckon consequences, good or ill?'.

Yet how deny that non-intent can kill?
It all came down to ringing you that day.
If I'd not phoned then you'd be living still.

Our acts produce all kinds of overspill,
Like twisted endings to a well-made play:
How reckon consequences, good or ill?

Perhaps you thought 'from now it's all downhill,
Why carry on?', but conscience has its say:
'If you'd not phoned then he'd be living still'.

A long life, episodes enough to fill
Ships' logs galore, now your dream-dossier.
How reckon consequences, good or ill?

Four wretched weeks in hospital, until
'Just leave me now': last message you'd convey.
If I'd not phoned then you'd be living still.
How reckon consequences, good or ill?

The Turing Test

*A computer would deserve to be called intelligent if it could deceive
a human into believing that it was human.*

*I believe that at the end of the century the use of words and general
educated opinion will have altered so much that one will be able to
speak of machines thinking without expecting to be contradicted.*

Alan Turing

Two ways this thing might go, this Turing Test.
Who's tested, who's the tester – how decide?
No algorithm shows the lead-role clear;
No help from *nous* if *techne* steals the show.

Not ours to know which party comes off best
When both take techno-savvy in their stride,
Both have (or are) the latest IT gear,
And both have hopped-up software on the go.

Seemed simple once: you questioned it and guessed,
Or figured out, if it was bona fide,
A living soul you were in touch with here,
Man or machine – human yourself, you'd know!

Six decades on and rate of change has messed
Things up: the computations multiplied
A zillion-fold, until it seems that we're
(Who 'we'?) just nodules in the data-flow.

The humans, feeling threatened, may invest
More heavily in fixing the divide,
Yet see how rapidly the techno-sphere
Expands to level up the quid pro quo.

They pile on bit-rates just to keep abreast,
Make expert protocols a source of pride,
Heap laurels on the software engineer,
And stand amazed as his dominions grow.

No wonder if the upshot of their quest
For brains of silicon that override
Our carbon networks is to conjure fear
Of what might buck the IQ ratio.

For it's the *Uebermensch* here manifest,
The future-shock they courted open-eyed,
The point where all their Faustian dreams appear
The promptings of some Boolean Mephisto.

Now they've erased the line they once transgressed,
Abjured the comforts of their users' guide,
And lost all cognisance of that frontier,
The line that Turing-testers hoped to toe.

It promised straightforward answers on request,
Hard borders drawn, hard cases clarified,
With every interface the sort you'd steer
Securely by and navigate just so.

Attempt it now: you'll find yourself hard-pressed
To spot the route those old plain-sailors plied,
Or know when mind begins to tack and veer
Across the line as border-guards lie low.

And you, the heirs of Turing, still addressed
By ghosts in your machine: how now abide
Their table-turning question when it's mere
Folk-prejudice keeps your ducks in a row?

For you're the spirit-conjurors possessed
Of a strange power that bids informants hide
Identities, not tilt the peer-to-peer
Non-personhood of Silicon Plateau;

And you're the neuromancers, cursed or blest,
Who have to hit on some means to provide
Us false assurance when the clues cohere
In ways unknown to Descartes, Kant & Co.

Too tough for hardline dualists to digest,
But true: it's now a question open wide
As to where 'human' ends and we draw near
The cyber-realm where physics may bestow

More sense of what the mystics once expressed,
That constant chafing at the cut-and-dried
Cartesian scheme of things that had mind jeer
At any debt to body it might owe.

It's this too quick, too soul-encumbered jest
That's now turned back by those who'd sooner side
With science even if it turns out queer,
Like giving old pan-psychism a throw.

That's why, as all our certitudes go west,
We're left with Turing's problem: how he tried,
And failed, to keep the two-way channels clear
Of cyborg cross-talk bouncing to and fro.

Out of Character

I am stupid, am I not? What more can I want? If you ask them who is brave . . , who is true . . , who is just . . . who is it they would trust with their lives? . . . they would say, Tuan Jim. And yet they can never know the real, real truth . . .

It is my belief that no man ever understands quite his own artful dodges to escape from the grim shadow of self-knowledge.

Joseph Conrad,
Lord Jim

It may even be the case that there is no such thing as character, no ordinary character traits of the sort people think there are, none of the usual moral virtues and vices.

Gilbert Harman

If personality were typically structured as evaluatively integrated associations of robust traits, it should be possible to observe very substantial consistency in behaviour. I therefore contend personality should be conceived of as fragmented: an evaluatively disintegrated association of situation-specific local traits.

John Doris

Quite 'out of character', his acting so.
You trust to habit, but the mask may slip.
The Dickens lot troop on and do their thing;
Snap choices ditch whole lives of heretofore.

Shaming yourself is one way it can go.
Lord Jim lived by the book but then jumped ship.
No life but has some alien self to spring;
No rest for him but sailing shore to shore.

Was that your secret-sharer there below
Or was it just a panic-stations blip?
Maybe, but if it's depth-reports they bring,
Those moments, then they're signs we can't ignore.

Some think the self's a standing debt we owe
To bygone selves, each personage a chip
Off that old building-block, or phrase we sing
Con anima yet strictly by the score.

For some it's more time's flow and counter-flow,
Its memory-glissades, that ease the grip
Of punctual selfhood by imagining
Times past revisited *une fois encore*.

The Proustian take has its own drawbacks, though,
As Marcel finds when selves and times-scales slip
Too far from sync and so require he cling
To cakes tea-dunked, then lodged in memory's store.

Two different ways of coming not to know
What's left of 'character' should something tip
The balance or your reputation swing
From guy they love to fellow they deplore.

It's down to figuring out the quid pro quo
When ratings lift, then take a sudden dip
As Marcel muses, or the constant sting
Of shame relived enacts the moral law.

No question: the resistless to-and-fro
Of time lost and retrieved affords a trip
Less arduous than the endless harrowing
Of self-reproach that Conrad's sailor bore.

Let's say that character's what takes a blow
When some till now disowned desire lets rip,
Or some long-stifled impulse has its fling
And conscience yields to instinct in the raw.

For *temps perdu* leaves ample room to stow
Past foibles, faults and follies, or to flip
From scene to scene so memory can string
Itself along and hide each moral flaw,

While there's no life-redemptive light to throw
On Jim's wracked 'character', no way to skip
That fateful moment, save by reckoning
With selves and consequences yet to draw.

Derrida's Cat: six sonnets

*When I play with my cat, who knows if I am not a pastime to her
more than she is to me?*

Michel de Montaigne,
'Apology for Raymond Sebond'

*The question is not, Can they reason? nor, Can they talk? but, Can
they suffer? Why should the law refuse its protection to any sensi-
tive being? . . . . The time will come when humanity will extend its
mantle over everything which breathes.*

Jeremy Bentham,
Introduction to the Principles of Morals and Legislation

*As with every bottomless gaze, as with the eyes of the other, the gaze
called 'animal' offers to my sight the abyssal limit of the human, .
. . the border-crossing from which vantage man dares to announce
himself to himself.*

Jacques Derrida,
The Animal That Therefore I Am

What's there to read in that impassive gaze?
The shared alterity, the he and she.
She sees me seeing how she sees me see.
It's a moot point: who's played with here, who plays?
No intercepting our communiqués;
No guessing what the call-sign, code or key
That lets two species channel-hop till we
Seem life-worlds momentarily in phase.
Too quick they are to count it fancy-bred,
A mere cat-lover's whim, that troubling thought
Of roles reversed that had the wily-wise
Montaigne so egregiously misled
As to praise animals by selling short
Those human creatures cherished in God's eyes.

Why then this strange confusion when she stays
To watch me after showering, looks at me
As anybody might who'd come to be
The silent sharer of my nights and days,
Yet shows herself unwilling now to raise
Her eyes or spare the level scrutiny,
As I stand naked, of a creature free
From shame or inhibition? When she lays
That gaze on me I feel what scripture said
The miscreants of Eden felt when taught
To clothe their parts in a more modest guise,
Do penance for those fig-leaves gladly shed,
And spurn all further invites to consort
With beastly kin not fit to recognise.

Such tortuous ways they went around, those heirs
Of Descartes, in the effort to persuade
Themselves that only humans made the grade,
Since any thought of critters having shares
In a life-world so far removed from theirs
Must show the same naivete displayed
By folk, pet-fanciers chiefly, who betrayed
Their misplaced love by risking all the snares
Of pure *bêtise*. Such ruses they deployed
To make it stick, that special-treatment rule
Whereby it's clear (let's say) my cat's the one
That's played with, not the player, since devoid
By nature of the wherewithal to fool
Around with me so she gets all the fun.

Yet still she's apt to catch me unawares,
To show (if showing's needed) how she's made
A fool of me and knowingly conveyed
What dupes we are, us humans, with our airs
And graces born of being kicked upstairs
By every creaturely trick of the trade
Those beasts deploy to see they're well repaid
For not too closely questioning who wears.

The trousers. It's their favour we've enjoyed,
Us lords-and-masters, nurtured in the school
Of cracked-up species eminence that's run
To save us getting downright paranoid
Should we suspect we've joined the talent-pool
Of those who strive that others' will be done.

From Descartes, Kant and Heidegger we hear
The same old tale: how critters occupy
A world or worlds apart from ours, a sty
Of deprivation, or an abject sphere
From whose far boundary they dimly peer
And, just as dimly, think to wonder why
This brute existence, born to live and die
On the wrong side of that one-way frontier.
Yet look again and maybe you'll discern
The slips, aporias, and hitherto
Unnoticed swerves of argument that show
How reading deconstructively can turn
The beast *v* human tables and undo
That mythic pecking-order, high to low.

Don't get me wrong: no greeting peer-to-peer
Or inter-species meeting eye-to-eye,
Us and 'the animals', since when we try
There's just too many things that interfere,
Among them all the myriad ways that we're
Fine-tuned to conspecifics, guided by
The aeons of evolution that supply
Our diverse kinds of head- and body-gear.
Still there's a useful lesson there to learn
From those philosophers: whenever you
Take difference to require that we bestow
Prized attributes one-sidedly you'll earn
Another put-down from the teeming zoo
Of swift retorts to Descartes, Kant & Co.

Epilogue: Husserl

First, anyone who seriously intends to become a philosopher must,
'once in his life', withdraw into himself and attempt, within him-
self, to overthrow and build anew all the sciences that, up to then,
he has been accepting. Philosophical wisdom is the philosopher's
personal affair. It must arise as his wisdom, as his self-acquired
knowledge tending toward universality, a knowledge for which he
can answer from the beginning, and at each step, by virtue of his
own absolute insights.

Edmund Husserl,
Cartesian Meditations

In our vital need science has nothing to say to us. It excludes in
principle precisely the questions which man, given over in our un-
happy times to the most portentous upheavals, finds the most burn-
ing: questions about the meaning or meaninglessness of this whole
human existence. Do not these questions, universal and necessary for
all men, demand universal reflections and answers based on ratio-
nal insight?

Husserl,
The Crisis of the European Sciences and
Transcendental Phenomenology

Life-world or certitude? When I review
My five decades and more of thought addressed
To problems unresolved by all the great
Philosophers from Plato down, it's those
Twin options that confront me and comprise
Whatever small advance my thinking made.

How should the life-world not receive its due,
That realm of shared experience manifest
In every social nuance, every state
Of mind made public, everything that goes

To prove, *contra* Descartes, that mental eyes
Alone won't help you scan the whole parade.

That's why my late work told them: better do
The *Lebenswelt* more justice – it's the test
Of whether your analyses should rate
'As vital work by striving to disclose
How all our mental episodes take rise
From worlds of sense too rich to be surveyed.

That's also why I warned them: each time you
New-style Cartesian rationalists invest
Yet more in your inflated estimate
Of cogito's domain you give your foes,
The raw empiricists, their fresh disguise
As hard-nosed realists when they briskly trade

On your wrong move. They take it as their cue
To tout empiricism as the best
Alternative to concepts as innate
Yet disembodied forms of cogito's
Mysterious power to access that which lies
Where phantoms loom as sense-impressions fade.

And so the tug-of-war yields neither crew
The least advantage while the upshot stressed
By their old deadlock is the dismal fate
Of any creed that fails to diagnose
That false dilemma. Else they'd recognize
This simple truth: that had both parties paid

Sufficient heed to all that might accrue
By way of knowledge tacitly accessed
From life-world contexts, then this whole debate
Would seem just one more replay of old woes
As minds expand to greet the open skies
Of thinking freed from Descartes' life-blockade.

Yet still it tempts me, that ideal that drew
My early project onward in its quest
For certitude, its will to shed the freight
Of cultural difference, and the way it chose
To question everything save what applies
To thoughts and judgments meriting the grade

'Shown valid necessarily since true
For transcendental subjects all possessed
Of faculties like ours'. Else we'd create
Each our own world, or everyone impose
Whichever paradigm they might devise
With no shared concept-scheme to call in aid

Where needed. Our whole world might go askew
Or our cognitions fail to keep abreast
Of things for want of concepts that dictate
What must be so for anyone who owes
Their life-world orientation to the ties
Of thought and sense-bestowal that I've laid

Out from first principles. It's only through
Such rigorous procedures that we'll wrest
Back logic, truth and reason from the gate
Of hell that gapes when thought turns comatose,
When rhetoric holds forth in logic's guise,
And ignorance heads up the hate-crusade.

My *Crisis* book confronts that hideous brew
Of hatred, fear and ignorance expressed
In every Nazi slogan used to bait
Us 'rootless intellectuals' for who knows
What crime if not that we might jeopardize
The rout of reason in this dark decade.

Hence my twin-pronged imperative, the two
Great tasks by which my soul has been possessed:
First, to resume and truly vindicate

The project of enquiry that arose
Way back with Descartes' sceptical surmise,
His saving twist on the eternal braid

Of doubt and reason, and – the task that grew
More urgent as skies darkened in the West
And reason's clock declared the hour was late –
Ensuring that this project not foreclose
On every living context that supplies
The stuff to bolster logic's palisade.

Such my resolve: unswervingly I'd hew
To both, much exercised but not distressed
By their persistent failure to equate
And thus resolve the paradox that shows
When some devoted commentator tries
To unify the duplex game I've played.

One blessing: they've no warrant to construe
Some primal script beneath my palimpsest,
Some *Ursprache* that's held to antedate
Philosophy itself since it bestows
(*Sic dixit* Heidegger) words-to-the-wise
Of sovereign import. This can't be conveyed

Unless we profs turn poets and eschew
All thoughts save those evoked at the behest
Of Greek or German with their special weight
Of depth-charged etymons revealed in prose,
Like his, whose vatic posturing defies
All sense and logic. His the accolade

Of having, by sheer genius, jumped the queue
From Plato to yours truly and addressed
Those questions over which we idlers skate
For want of acumen. Not otiose,
That depth-semantic stuff he'd improvise,
But all too redolent of words that swayed

The German *Volk* to greet the Nazi coup
As likewise honoring a great bequest
Too long withheld by those who'd mis-translate
Its noble destiny. I held my nose
Too long in fear that, should I criticize
My own star student Heidegger, then they'd

Ascribe it to an old man's need to woo
New followers, get some grievance off his chest,
Or settle scores. No: it's to put them straight –
My exegetes – on why my thinking goes
Such lengthy ways around to mobilize
Its powers against the bacillus that preyed

On Martin's thought and made its grand debut
In Hitler's Nuremberg. I'll leave the rest
To those successors who'll not hesitate
To warn when mere afflatus overthrows
The lucid vigil that good thinkers prize
For its life-world revealing light and shade.

About the Author

Christopher Norris is Emeritus Professor in Philosophy at the University of Cardiff where he taught English Literature until 1991 and then moved over into Philosophy via his special interests in literary theory and modern Continental thought. He has published more than thirty books on topics in philosophy, literary theory, the history of ideas, cultural politics, and musical criticism. Norris's early work on the critic and poet William Empson has remained a major point of reference, as have his studies of Spinoza, Derrida, Paul de Man, Hilary Putnam, and Alain Badiou. His books on deconstruction were among the first to introduce Derrida's thought to an Anglophone readership and to establish its jointly philosophical and literary bearings. He has also made important contributions to current debates in philosophy of science, including books about scientific realism, quantum mechanics, and the self-refuting character of anti-realist or relativist approaches. More recently he has turned to writing poetry and verse-essays which often draw on those earlier interests to generate a new kind of creative writing focused on the various complex intersections of imaginative, fictive, scholarly, philosophical, and speculative thought. He has lectured, taught and held visiting appointments at many universities around the world.

CPSIA information can be obtained
at www.ICGtesting.com
Printed in the USA
FSHW020955160520
70046FS